The Book of Creation

Books by J. Philip Newell published by Paulist Press

Celtic Prayers from Iona

Listening to the Heartbeat of God: A Celtic Spirituality

One Foot in Eden: A Celtic View of the Stages of Life

The Book of Creation

The Book of Creation

An Introduction to Celtic Spirituality

J. Philip Newell

PAULIST PRESS
New York • Mahwah, N.J.

Published by arrangement with Canterbury Press, 181 Queen Victoria Street, London EC4V 4DD.

Illustrations by Shirley Norman.

Library of Congress Cataloging-in-Publication Data

Newell, J. Philip.
   The book of creation : an introduction to Celtic spirituality / by J. Philip Newell.
       p. cm. — (Rhythm of life (New York, N.Y.))
   Includes bibliographical references.
   ISBN 0-8091-3899-9 (alk. paper)
   1. Spirituality—Celtic Church.   2. Creation—History of doctrines. I. Title. II. Series.
BR748 .N45 1999
248´.089´916—dc21   99-34545
                                                                      CIP

Published by Paulist Press
997 Macarthur Boulevard
Mahwah, New Jersey 07430

www.paulistpress.com

Printed and bound in the
United States of America

Contents

The Reverend J. Philip Newell, born in Canada in 1953, is Warden of Spirituality for the Anglican Diocese of Portsmouth, England. He is a Church of Scotland minister who has served at St. Giles' Cathedral, Edinburgh, and as Warden of Iona Abbey. His doctrinal research at the University of Edinburgh was in Scottish spirituality, and since then he has played a significant role on both sides of the Atlantic in the recovery of the Celtic tradition for today. He resides in Portsmouth with his wife, Alison, and their four children.

Preface

My earliest memories of creation are primarily of light. They come to me in a kaleidoscope of recollection, of light reflecting off the waters of northern Canadian lakes where I spent time as a boy or of the clarity of the night skies above those same waters. I often would sit mesmerized by the sun's setting colours or by the immediacy of starlight in the dark. I do not believe that I am unusual in this, nor do I think that the wildness of the context was necessary to the depth of the impression, for I also remember light in the city, glistening off the metallic chrome of cars or dappling through the white curtains of my nursery window. In fact it is important that these memories are not unique, for the experience of the light that is in creation is a universal gift.

This is why the Celtic tradition of spirituality is so significant to me. Its starting-point is not an experience that separates one group of people from another but a gift that we all have been given. As my teacher, Noel O'Donoghue, used to say, 'In the beginning was the gift, and the gift was with God, and the gift was God.' In the Celtic tradition the gift of creation is essentially a self-giving of God.

Writing this book has awakened in me memories of my experience of that continuous gift and of the people with whom I have shared it. I am thinking not just of the men and women whom I have known and loved but of the people who remain nameless to me but alongside whom I have received the same morning light and the same burst of colour from the earth. The gift of creation is our common ground, even though for so many people for so much of the time it is a neglected gift or a gift shrouded in pain.

There are a number of people whom I especially would like to thank. Kenneth White, the Scottish poet, whose work I became familiar with only a few years ago, has made a deep impression on me. To discover poetry that gives voice to some of one's deepest intuitions is an experience not often given in life. And to find that he too was an appreciator of Celtic teachers like Pelagius and Eriugena confirmed in me a sense of the importance of rediscovering and making known the riches of this tradition.

Belatedly I would like to thank Elspeth and Gordon Strachan who years ago in Edinburgh were so supportive of me during my doctoral research on the Celtic teacher Alexander Scott. It has only been in the writing of this book that I have appreciated fully the contribution of Scott towards the recovery of a spirituality that is integrated with the mystery of creation. Gordon and Elspeth, who for over twenty years have been on the cutting edge of such a recovery in Scotland, have appreciated this all along.

Many people in Portsmouth diocese have been encouragers of the work that has gone into this book. Particularly I would like to thank those who were part of the Epiphany series at St Thomas's Cathedral, where the first 'dry run' of this material was offered. The shared meditations in the cathedral, and our continued discussions in the pub across the road, enriched the process. The setting of the series in the east end of the cathedral was just right, thanks to the generous provision of the Provost and Chapter and the imagination of the vergers.

I would especially like to thank Bishop Graham Chadwick for asking me to write this volume in the *Rhythm of Life* series for Canterbury Press. One of his many gifts is the ability to ask gently with a persuasive power that is difficult to resist. It has enabled him over his few years at Sarum College, Salisbury, as Director of the Institute for Christian Spirituality, to create an important resource for spirituality in southern England. He graciously embodies in his life the sorts of things he asks other people to write and talk about.

As with most of the important creativities in my life, Alison, my wife, has played a vital role. On this occasion I found that she already had arrived at most of the places of new perspective to which I was travelling, but by different roads. When occasionally I am humble enough to recognize her influence I am very thankful.

J. Philip Newell
St John's House
June 1998

To Creativity
and the dancing of my daughter,
Kirsten Margaret Iona

Introduction

The Scottish poet Kenneth White, in his poem 'Letter from Harris',[1] writes,

> I open the book
> and the words
> fly out of the page

The book that he is referring to is creation. It is, as one Celtic teacher says, 'the grand volume of God's utterance'.[2] That is where the Creator speaks, in and through all that has been created. In our Western Christian inheritance we have received a sense of what it means to listen for the Word of God in the Scriptures. The Word is understood as deeper than the words themselves. It is 'living and active', as the Bible says, 'sharper than any two-edged sword', and capable of piercing our hearts with truth.[3] But what does it mean to listen for the Word of God in creation? And where does this emphasis come from?

It is important to understand that the spirituality of Celtic Christianity did not spring out of nowhere. Its roots reach deep into the mysticism of St John the Evangelist in the New Testament and even further back into the Wisdom tradition of the Old Testament. The Book of Wisdom, for instance, says that we are made 'in the image of God's nature' and that wisdom has been 'the fashioner of what exists'.[4] Where do we look, therefore, to learn of God? It is not away from ourselves and away from creation, but deep within all that has life. That is where the truth of God is hidden, like treasure buried in a field.

Similarly, St John says that 'in the beginning was the Word' and that all things have come into being through the Word.[5] This is to say that essentially all life is an expression of God. We have been uttered into being. To learn of God, therefore, is to listen to the heart of life. Part of the Celtic tradition's love of St John, whom it affectionately refers to as 'John of Love' or 'John the Beloved', was its memory of him as the one who leaned against Jesus at the last supper.[6] He is said to have heard the heartbeat of God. Thus St John became a symbol of listening for the life of God, both within ourselves and within all creation.[7] In listening within we will hear falseness and confusion, selfishness and violence of heart, but deeper still is the Love that utters all things into being.

Christianity first appeared among the Celts in the second century, if not earlier. By this point in time they were living 'on the edge of the habitable world', as Britain and Ireland were then regarded.[8] At an earlier stage, from about the fifth century BC, the Celts had formed something of an 'empire' that stretched right across Europe into Asia Minor. The expansion of Roman domination, however, pushed the Celts further and further west, until by the middle of the first century AD the Roman army had occupied many of the Celtic kingdoms of Britain. It was during the Roman occupation that Christianity first came to the Celts, possibly through the ministrations of individual converts in the Roman army.

It is not, however, until late in the fourth century that distinct characteristics of Celtic Christianity begin to emerge. The first teacher of note in the Celtic tradition was a monk by the name of Pelagius, which in Welsh was rendered 'Morgan' or 'Morien'. For over 1500 years his name has been identified with the heresy 'Pelagianism', condemned for its supposed teaching that humanity is capable of saving itself without the aid of divine grace. As we shall see, Pelagius did not teach this. Like the Wisdom tradition of the Old Testament and the perspective of St John in the New Testament, he emphasized that what is deepest in us is the image of God. God's wisdom is born with us 'in the womb', as Ecclesiasticus says,[9] or, as St John says, in us is 'the true light that enlightens everyone coming into the world'.[10] Sin has buried the beauty of God's image, but not erased it. The gospel is given to uncover the hidden wealth of God that has been planted in the depths of our human nature. Pelagius was misinterpreted as saying that we therefore do not need grace. Rather, in the Celtic tradition both grace and nature are celebrated as gifts of God. The gift of grace is given to restore us to the essential well-being of the gift of nature.

A long theological controversy between Pelagius and Augustine of Hippo resulted eventually in Pelagius's excommunication – not that it was always clear which way the judgement of Rome would fall. The Church in the Roman world was still feeling its way towards its theological understanding of human nature. It had not yet defined the doctrine of 'original sin', whereby humanity is declared essentially sinful. That Pelagius in the end was banned from the Roman Empire and excommunicated by the Bishop of Rome should not prejudge for us the value of what this early Celtic teacher was saying. The impression we have been given is that he was simply a one-off heretic. The reality is that he was reflecting the spirituality of the young British Church. Just as Luther, who in the sixteenth century was declared a 'heretic' by Rome, in fact was giving voice to spiritual perceptions that were arising in people throughout much of Europe, so Pelagius 'the heretic' was articulating a spirituality that reflected the development of British Christianity in the fourth century.

Around the same time as Pelagius's excommunication, the Roman occupying army withdrew to the continent in an attempt to stem the flow of barbarian invasions into central and southern Europe. The Romans were never able to recover Britain. The result was nearly 200 years of significant separation between the Celtic mission of the Church and the Roman mission. This was an important stage in the development of Celtic spirituality, for now British Christianity was relatively free from Roman domination. During the fifth and sixth centuries, which were marked by a large-scale conversion to Christianity in Ireland and Britain, the Celtic mission continued its emphasis on the image of God at the heart of the human and its conviction of the essential goodness of creation. Alongside these characteristics were other distinct features of the Celtic tradition, such as clerical marriage and the inclusion of women in the leadership of the Church.

At the same time the Roman tradition was hardening its accentuation of Augustine's doctrine of total human depravity along with the belief that creation is essentially flawed. The grace of God was seen as over and against nature, not as restoring humanity and creation to their God-given natural goodness. Similarly, its mission was viewed as taking the light of God into an essentially dark world. The Celtic mission, on the other hand, in line with the mysticism of St John, emphasized the truth that God is 'the light of life'.[11] Repentance, therefore, was a turning to what is most deeply planted within us, the light that has not been overcome by the darkness. Alongside these characteristics of the Roman mission was a growing insistence on clerical celibacy and the exclusion of women from positions of leadership within the Church.

Holding all of this together in the Roman mission, and giving leadership to it, was the growing consolidation of papal power. Uniformity was being enforced from the centre. The Celtic mission, conversely, had no central organizing force, and consequently there was considerable variation in liturgical practice and monastic rules. While a diocesan model had been attempted in the early mission of St Patrick, the Celtic kingdoms were largely agricultural. A lack of town structure rendered the diocesan model of mission unworkable. By the beginning of the sixth century, Celtic Christianity was wholly monastic in its structure. It consisted of a loose federation of monastic communities, each monastery owing obedience to its mother-house. It was in this context that women such as St Bride of Kildare headed up 'families' of monastic communities, many of which were 'double' monasteries in which men and women pursued lives of monastic discipline alongside one another.

When the Roman mission to Britain was launched in 597 under the leadership of Augustine of Canterbury, it is not surprising that conflict ensued. The Celtic missions of the sixth century had burst forth from Ireland under the leadership of St Columba and others with a tremendous energy and flowering of culture. In the latter half of the century they stretched from the holy islands of Iona and Lindisfarne into the southern kingdoms of the Angles and Saxons. When the Roman and Celtic missions met there was considerable disagreement.

At one level the conflicts that emerged appear superficial, such as the dating of Easter and the style of clerical tonsure. At a deeper level, however, the discord was between two radically different ways of seeing. Part of the Roman unease about the Celtic tonsure was that it had been the

druidic tonsure. Typical of the Celtic mission was the practice of baptizing religious symbols and teachings from the
pre-Christian nature mysticism. Columba, for instance,
referred to Christ as his druid. Similarly many of the holy
sites and oak groves were transformed into monastic bases
for Christian mission. Christ was preached as the fulfilment
of everything that was true, including the wisdom of the
tradition that preceded Christianity in Celtic Britain.

The conflict between the two missions led eventually to
the Synod of Whitby in 664. The representatives of the
Celtic mission argued from the authority of St John whom,
they said, was 'especially loved by our Lord'.[12] The Roman
mission, on the other hand, appealed to the authority of
St Peter as 'the most blessed Prince of the Apostles' to
whom Jesus had said, 'You are Peter, and on this rock I
will build my church.'[13] The outcome of the synod was a
judgement against the Celtic mission.

The tragedy of Whitby was not that the way of Peter
was affirmed but rather that the way of John began to be
displaced in the spirituality of the British Church. Celtic
monastic communities were now replaced by Benedictine
monasteries, and a strict uniformity to Rome was enforced.
On the holy island of Lindisfarne in Northumbria, where
the Celtic community had worshipped outside, around
high-standing crosses or in simple wooden structures, the
four stone walls of a Roman church were built. It symbolized the ascendancy of a religious tradition that increasingly was to separate the mystery of God from the mystery
of creation. More and more the 'holy' place was identified
with the sanctuary of the church rather than the sanctuary
of earth, sea and sky.

The decree of Whitby did not suddenly change the face
of British Christianity. For hundreds of years there were
pockets of resistance to the Roman mission, notably in

Devon, Cornwall and Scotland. On Iona the Celtic monastic community was not finally dispersed until the building of the thirteenth-century Benedictine Abbey. The period of resistance was marked by some of the greatest creative achievements of the Celtic tradition. The beautiful illumination of gospel manuscripts, such as *The Book of Kells*, and the high-standing crosses that incorporated scripture imagery on one side and creation imagery on the other reached their peak of artistic expression during these centuries. The general picture throughout Britain and Ireland, however, was of gradual conformity to the Roman mission.

As the outward structure of the Celtic mission fragmented, the tradition found a continuity of expression in the fields of art and education. Celtic teachers, relatively free from ecclesiastical censure, now became the principal spokesmen of the spiritual truths that had no formal church home. Perhaps the greatest of these was the ninth-century Irish teacher, John Scotus Eriugena. He taught that God is the 'Life Force' within all things.[14] 'Therefore every visible and invisible creature', he said, 'can be called a theophany.'[15] All life manifests something of the One who is the essence of life. The two primary modes of God's self-revelation, he said, are the Bible and creation: 'Through the letters of Scripture and the species of creature' the eternal Light is revealed.[16] Eriugena, like many Celtic teachers before and after him, was accused of pantheism. Eventually his writings were condemned by Rome, but not until long after his death.

Alongside the writings of Eriugena and the work of countless Irish teachers throughout Western Europe, the insights of Celtic spirituality were kept alive in Britain and Ireland through the poetry and prayers of the people. Pre-Christian Celtic culture had been characterized by a love of memory and eloquence. It was understood that the spoken

word held more power than physical might. The teachings
and wisdom of this pre-literate culture had been orally
transmitted and memorized in verse form. The prizing of
memory and eloquence continued into the Christian era.
After the demise of the Celtic mission the riches of its
spirituality were safeguarded in the teachings of an oral
tradition passed down among the laity. It was like a spiritual resistance movement. For centuries one generation
would impart to the next the prayers that had their origin
in the early centuries of Celtic Christianity. These were
prayers of daily life. They were sung or chanted at the
rising of the sun and at its setting or in the midst of daily
work and routine. They were uttered at the birth of a child
or at the deathbed of a loved one. God was celebrated as
the Life within all life. Creation was seen as the dwelling
place of God.

Again the Celtic tradition met with resistance. Increasingly, and especially after the sixteenth-century
Reformation in Britain, the reciting of these prayers was
discouraged and even banned. They were regarded as pan-
theistic and pagan in origin. In Scotland the combination of
religious persecution and the nineteenth-century Highland
clearances, in which thousands of families were torn from
their ancestral lands to make room for large-scale sheep
farming, resulted in a fragmentation of Celtic culture and
loss of collective memory. The oral tradition began to be
lost. Attempts were made to transcribe and collect the
prayers, such as Alexander Carmichael's *Carmina Gadelica*
in Scotland and Douglas Hyde's *Religious Songs of Connacht* in Ireland.[17] These ensured that written records of
some of the prayers were preserved, but by the twentieth
century their living use had virtually disappeared.

This did not, however, represent the death of the Celtic
tradition. Carmichael and Hyde were part of a revival of

Celtic art and literature, and others were finding new ways to express the spirituality of the tradition. George Mac-Donald, the Scottish novelist, was weaving the insights of the Celtic tradition into his widely read short stories and novels. Similarly, his teacher, the Scottish mystic Alexander Scott, was retrieving the creation emphasis of Celtic spirituality and attempting to integrate it into the theology of nineteenth-century British Christianity. Creation, said Scott, is 'a transparency through which a light of God is seen'.[18] He was condemned for heresy by the Church of Scotland, and once again there were accusations of pantheism. But a change was coming.

The twentieth century has brought not only a growing toleration of the Celtic tradition but increasingly a depth of appreciation for its spiritual riches and their applicability for today. This has occurred not only on the edge of the Church but within it as well. Lord MacLeod, for instance, the founder of the Iona Community in the Hebrides, represented in his spirituality a combination of Celtic mystical perspective and deep personal commitment to the Scottish Church. As he said in one of his prayers, 'In all created things Thou art there.'[19] This led him towards not only a type of creation mysticism and ecological concern but also an identification of Christ with the poor and a commitment to working for justice and non-violence in the cities of Scotland.

The modern-day resurgence of interest in all matters Celtic has taken many forms, from dance and music through arts and craft to prayers and poetry. Some of these are more true to the history of the Celtic tradition than others. Most of them, however, reflect the desire that countless numbers of people in the Western world are becoming aware of: the desire to reintegrate our lives and our spirituality with the mystery of creation. Kenneth

White, one of the greatest English-speaking poets of the late twentieth century, gives powerful expression to this desire in his poetry. In 'North Roads, South Roads' he describes his journey as being,

> with a bible in one hand
> a lump of quartz in the other[20]

It speaks of the longing that people are experiencing throughout the Western world for a wholeness that will hold together their spirituality with their love of creation.

One of the gaps in the resurgence of interest in Celtic spirituality is the absence of a well-defined method of meditation. The Celtic tradition is perceived widely as conveying a general sense of reverence for creation. It is not known, however, for offering specific methods of awareness. This book attempts to be a guide in the practice of Celtic spirituality and meditation. Each chapter, by reflecting on one of the days of creation in the Book of Genesis, explores a different aspect of creation as 'theophany' or 'manifestation of God'. And at the end of each chapter there is a meditation exercise that applies the Celtic tradition's twin-love of scripture and creation. It is a way of listening in stereo, as it were, to the book of scripture and the book of creation.

Among the few manuscripts mentioned with frequency in the old Celtic monasteries was Cassian's *Conferences*. Cassian was a fifth-century monk who studied the monasticism of the Egyptian desert and recorded a method of meditation that was derived from the early Desert Fathers. It bears resemblance to, and was likely influenced by, the Eastern mantra method of prayer whereby inner stillness is achieved through the repetition of words or phrases. The Scriptures say, 'Be still, and know that I am God.'[21] All of the great traditions of meditation offer simple ways of being still in order to be more aware. The method that Cassian describes was adapted by Western monasticism into a discipline of prayer that came to be known as *lectio divina*. This consists of three parts: the recalling of words from Scripture; the repeating of these words as a way of being still; and then the offering of prayer from the heart.

In the Celtic tradition Cassian's method can be applied to the book of creation as well as the book of scripture. As part of the meditation exercise at the end of each chapter there is a recalling of words from scripture as well as images from creation. An inner repetition of these is a way of being still and attentive at levels deeper than thought. Kenneth White describes an awareness of the essence of life as

> taking off the clothes of the mind
> and making love
> to the body of reality[22]

My hope for this book is that it will enrich our thoughts and our creativities and, more importantly, our loving of the Mystery and of one another.

Acknowledgements

Bible quotations are from the New Revised Standard Version (NRSV) 1989.

The publisher acknowledges with thanks permission to reproduce extracts from the following publications:

Kenneth White, *The Bird Path: Collected Longer Poems*, Mainstream Publishing, 1989.

John Scotus Eriugena, *Periphyseon (The Division of Nature)*, Editions Bellarmin, 1987.

B. R. Rees (ed.), *The Letters of Pelagius and his Followers*, Boydell Press, 1991.

THE
FIRST DAY:
THE
LIGHT OF
GOD

The First Day:
The Light of God

And God said, 'Let there be light'; and there was light. (Genesis 1:3)

John Scotus Eriugena, the ninth-century Celtic teacher, in reflecting on the 'seven days' of creation in the Book of Genesis, taught that it is not a chronological account of the making of the earth. Rather, it is a meditation on the ever-present mystery of creation. To say that light is created on the first day is to say that light is at the heart of life. It is the beginning of creation in the sense that it is the essence or centre from which life proceeds. At the heart of all that has life is the light of God. This is a fundamental belief of the Celtic tradition.

St John the Evangelist's way of putting it is to speak of this light as 'the light of life'[1] or 'the light that enlightens everyone coming into the world'.[2] Nothing has life apart from this light. It dapples through the whole of creation. It is within the brilliance of the morning sun and the whiteness of the moon at night. It issues forth in all that grows from the ground and in the life that shines from the eyes of any living creature. This is not to pretend that there are not also terrible darknesses deep within us and in the whole of creation. Rather it is to say that the light is deeper still and that it emanates from the love of God.

Eriugena also saw, in a way that anticipated the modern scientific understanding of life in its inter-relatedness, that all creation was made together. He was not, of course, meaning that all things became visible at once, but rather that all life is rooted in the light of the 'first day'. In time God draws forth from that pool of light the countless streams of earth's life-forms and species. Since the very beginning of creation we and all life have been hidden in 'the secret folds of nature', says Eriugena, waiting for the time of our manifestation.[3] In other words, the light of the first day is the source of our life and of all life.

This is comparable to aspects of the new physics in which the initial speck of matter exploding at the universe's birth is regarded as containing all that is to come. One modern physicist describes the unfolding of the universe over millions of years as the explication of what was implicated in its first moment.[4] Eriugena's point, which is characteristic of the Celtic tradition at every stage in its development, is that all life is interwoven, past and present, seen and unseen. Not only is the life of one species interdependent on the life of another, but the whole fabric of creation is woven through with the thread of God's light. It is like a material shot through with silk. If somehow this thread were removed the whole of creation would unravel.

Eriugena uses the image of lines coming out of the centre of a circle. The further one proceeds from the central point the more divergent the lines appear. To trace each radius back to its starting-point, however, is to find the place of common origin. Similarly the heart of all life is the light of God. The more deeply we move in relation to any created thing the closer we approach 'the divine brilliance' at the centre.[5] That light may have become covered over by all sorts of confusion and wrongdoing. Dark streaks of sin and suffering reach deep into the body of creation, but at its heart remains the 'brilliance' that has not been overcome by the darkness. It is to this light that we are called to be reconnected, both within ourselves and in all things.

Much later in the Celtic tradition, George MacLeod, the founder of the modern-day Iona Community, spoke of Christ as 'vibrant in the material world, not just in the spiritual world'.[6] This was to refuse to divide dualistically *see* the spiritual from the material. It was also to assert that the essence of life, both visible and invisible, is the light of God. As we shall find again and again in the Celtic continuity over the centuries, this has profoundly affected the way in which the matter of creation is responded to, whether that is the matter of earth's body or the bodies of women, men and human communities. Long before the beginnings of twentieth-century ecological consciousness the Celtic tradition was saying with George MacLeod that 'matter matters', because woven through the physical strands of the universe is the light that was in the beginning. What we do to ourselves and what we do to the cosmos is part of such a spirituality.

The Celtic poet Kenneth White, known for his earth-related writings, or what he calls 'geopoetics', speaks of the 'whiteness' that is at the core of reality. It is a whiteness written in creation 'like birch bark', he says, or 'like wave crest'.[7] It glistens in the life of the earth and sea and skies. We may lose sight of it, or cut ourselves off from it, to the extent that we cease to believe that it is there, yet the light continues to shine. It is 'the fire-body' from which all life proceeds.[8]

The light of the first day, of course, is not to be confused with the lights of the fourth day. The great luminaries of the sky, the sun, moon and stars come forth from the light that was in the beginning, but so does the earth and its

waters and the whole of creation. The light of the first
day is an invisible 'fiery power', says Eriugena.[9] From that
inaccessible light of God all life comes forth, whether that
be the morning light of the burning sun, the yellow brilliance of a sunflower growing from the dark ground or the
glow of a starfish emerging in the depths of the sea. It is
the light within all life, or, as George MacLeod says, the
'Sun behind all suns'.[10] Our eyes cannot see it, nor can
human thought nor imagination grasp it. Contemplating
the light that is at the heart of life takes us 'beyond signs',
says White,

> into the light
> that is not the sun[11]

Here we are led towards what Eriugena calls the 'darkness'
or unknowableness of God's light.[12]

As the nineteenth-century Celtic teacher Alexander Scott
said, the light of God in all things is not only 'bright', it
is 'awful'.[13] It proceeds from a place that is womb-like in
its dark, inaccessible mystery. We may feel ourselves
touched by it in the light of the sun or the moon, or experience it within ourselves moving us to passion and creativity, but it can neither be seen nor comprehended. 'The
Divine Dark', says Eriugena, 'excels every intellect.'[14] It
defies definition. Part of what we need to recover in our
Western religious traditions is not only a sharper sense of
the glory of God's light flooding the world of creation but
an awareness always that it issues forth from a realm that
is frighteningly beyond anything that we are capable of
knowing or gazing into.

This tension was preserved in the Celtic tradition by
Eriugena when he taught that God shows himself in all
things but can be known in nothing. He is in that sense
'Nothing', and yet shows himself in everything.[15] In the

strength of the wind, in the goodness of what grows from the ground, in the light of the waters, in the wild roaring of a bear, in the innocent beauty of a child, God expresses himself. He is 'the Being on which all being rests', as Scott says.[16] And yet God can never be known. He is always more than the wind and the waters, other than the bear and the child, greater than thought and image. While Eriugena taught that the light of life is a theophany or showing of God, God is always more than that light. Though invisible, it is a created light and can never truly reveal the Uncreated. God expresses the light of creation into being and yet is beyond creation; he is simultaneously immanent to the universe and transcendent to it. Thus the Celtic tradition points to the Mystery as both brilliance and darkness. The nineteenth-century Scottish novelist, George MacDonald, claimed that it is only the shadows of God's light that we glimpse in the life of creation and in ourselves.

Although the light of life is an invisible light, it is the life-giving stream that flows throughout the whole of the visible universe. If somehow that flow of light were to be dammed up, all things would cease to exist. Eriugena interprets the word *theos* (God) as derived from the verb *theo* (He who runs), for God 'runs throughout all things and never stays but by His running fills out all things'.[17] Kenneth White refers to it as the 'glow-flow' that courses through the veins of life.[18] And what the 'flow' desires, he says, is not philosophical and scientific analysis,

> it wants you
> to get into the flow[19]

God is to be found not by stepping aside from the flow of daily life into religious moments and environments, or by looking away from creation to a spiritual realm beyond, but rather by entering attentively the depths of the present moment. There we will find God, wherever we may be and whatever we may be doing. Our times of religious observation and meditative practice are not alternatives to encountering God in the ever-flowing stream of life. Rather they are moments of preparing ourselves to be alert to the One who is always and everywhere present, closer to us than we are to ourselves.

George MacLeod spoke of the light of God as 'warming and moving all Creation'. As he says in one of his prayers,

> The grass is vibrant,
> The rocks pulsate.
> All is in flux; turn but a stone and an angel moves.[20]

It is not as if creation somehow exists independently of God, the impression we have received too often from a mechanistic world-view, and that God only periodically chooses to express himself through it. That would be to say that God is like an artist who has made a violin that he only occasionally plays. The rising of the sun each morning is the expression of God, as is the beauty of the moon at night. The sun and the moon and the whole of creation do not exist apart from the flow of God's light. Its 'very effusion or extension or running', says Eriugena, 'precedes all things and is the cause of the existence of all things and is all things'.[21]

There is a tendency to romanticize the Celtic tradition's sense of the presence of God in all that is. We more readily look to the beauty of a Hebridean sunset, for instance, or to the array of dawn colour over vast stretches of sea than to the light of life in the city or in the places and people whom we find it difficult to view as bearers of God's brilliance. But, as Kenneth White writes:

the loveliness is everywhere
even
in the ugliest
and most hostile environment
the loveliness is everywhere
at the turning of a corner
in the eyes
and on the lips
of a stranger
in the emptiest areas
where is no place for hope
and only death
invites the heart
the loveliness is there
it emerges
incomprehensible
inexplicable
it rises in its own reality
and what we must learn is
how to receive it
into ours[22]

The Celtic tradition invites us to look with the inner eye. In all people, in all places, in every created thing the light of God is shining. It may lie buried and forgotten under layers of darkness and distortion but it is there waiting to be recovered.

As George MacLeod says in one of his prayers, 'Show to us the glory in the grey'.[23] It is a looking for the light of God in the most ordinary, and even dullest, of contexts. In MacLeod's case it was a search that led him into the worst slums of Glasgow in the 'Hungry Thirties', there to affirm the presence of light among some of the most economically destitute and socially neglected men and women of Scotland. Similarly, in 'Walking the Coast', Kenneth White writes of the glow that can be found within the apparent dullness of nature:

> the pebble of rough
> and unprepossessing stone
> the harsh dull case
> splits open
> to reveal
> the lovely agate crystal
> the boulder
> cut asunder
> shows a blue-gleaming layer of amethyst –
> there is a principle
> of beauty and order
> at the heart of chaos
> within life there is life[24]

What are the 'greynesses' and 'hard dull cases' of our lives, whether that be in our environments and communities, or in ourselves and relationships, deeper than which we may look to recover a sense of the light and beauty of the first day?

The Celtic tradition often portrays grace as washing away the things that obscure the essential goodness of life. The light that was in the beginning still glows at the heart of life but we do not see its full brilliance. 'It was to bring human nature back to this vision that the Incarnate Word of God descended,' writes Eriugena, 'sweeping away the shadows of false phantasies, opening the eyes of the mind, showing Himself in all things.'[25] Grace is like a cleansing rain over the landscape of life, followed by a sunlight that restores our vision. As Kenneth White writes,

the sky has broken
and the earth
sea-washed
is all diamond[26]

Rather than the dullness or darkness that we have feared
to be deepest in creation and in ourselves, we find, as
St John writes, that 'the light shines in the darkness, and
the darkness has not overcome it'.[27]

The reality for most of us much of the time, however,
is that we live as 'fugitives from the true light'.[28] Divorced
from the brilliance of the first day we live in a type of exile
from our true selves and from what is deepest in creation.
We may be adept at denying the yearnings that stir within
us for that light, and we may prefer to follow distractions
at the surface of life rather than address the deep longings
that arise from the heart of who we are, but there is within
each of us what Alexander Scott calls a 'homesickness'.[29]
It is a desire to be recollected to what is 'first' or deepest
in life.

The extent to which as individuals and societies we have
cut ourselves off from the light at the heart of life will be
the extent to which we must journey to recover it. Our
path of return will take us into dimensions of the mystery
of life and of ourselves that we may not have been conscious of. As Kenneth White says, 'only long miles of
strangeness can lead us to our home'.[30] We all know what
it is like to feel strange in unfamiliar territory, or at times
to feel distant from ourselves when we have lived in ways
that betray our true depths. In the Celtic tradition redemption is the journey of being reconnected to the light of God
within. It is a journey home that takes us through what
seems like unknown land.

It is not that God has been absent from us but that we

have been absent from God, and therefore from the light that is within us and at the centre of all life. God's light is the very root of life. Too often in our Western religious traditions we have been given the impression that sin has had the power to undo what God has woven into the very fabric of being. Redemption in such models of spirituality is about light coming from afar to shine in what is essentially dark. In the Celtic tradition, on the other hand, redemption is about light being liberated from the heart of creation and from the essence of who we are. It has not been overcome by darkness. Rather, the light is held in terrible bondages within us, waiting to be set free.

This is the image powerfully portrayed in the beautiful 'Christmas Carol' of the Hebridean collection of prayers and poems known as the *Carmina Gadelica*:

> This is the long night, . . .
> It will snow and it will drift, . . .
> White snow there will be till day, . . .
> White moon there will be till morn, . . .
> This night is the eve of the Great Nativity, . . .
> This night is born Mary Virgin's Son, . . .
> This night is born Jesus, Son of the King of glory, . . .
> This night is born to us the root of our joy, . . .
> This night gleamed the sun of the mountains high, . . .
> This night gleamed sea and shore together, . . .
> This night was born Christ the King of greatness, . . .
> Ere it was heard that the Glory was come, . . .
> Heard was the wave upon the strand, . . .
> Ere 'twas heard that His foot had reached the
>   earth, . . .
> Heard was the song of the angels glorious, . . .
> This night is the long night, . . .
> Glowed to Him wood and tree,

Glowed to Him mount and sea,
Glowed to Him land and plain,
When that His foot was come to earth.[31] *Xmas* .

When the foot of the redeemer touches the earth, the light within creation glows to him in response. Redemption is not the bringing of light to a creation that is essentially dark, but rather the liberating of light from the heart of life.

An important feature of Celtic spirituality, that appears again and again in a variety of ways over the centuries, is the refusal to divorce the gift of nature from the gift of grace. Both are seen as of God. The former, says Eriugena, is the gift of 'being' that God has given us, rooted in the light of the first day. The latter is the gift of 'well-being'.[32] It restores us or reconnects us to the light of life. The *NB.* mysteries of creation and redemption are one. They are not in opposition to each other. Holding them together allows for a celebration of the essential goodness of life as a gift from God, while at the same time being aware of the power of evil and of our need to be set free from its bondage.

In a meditation on the light that is at the heart of life, I saw myself walking further and further down a spiral staircase into the darkness of the earth. In my hand was a small candle that threw enough light for me to be able to see a few steps at a time. In the darkness I gradually became aware of a great fire of light that was deeper than the darkness. Eventually I saw that it was a roaring blaze and knew that the little light in my hand was a mere spark of the great fire to lead me to itself. George MacDonald calls this 'the central fire of the universe'.[33]

In one of the prayers from the *Carmina Gadelica* Jesus is called 'Son of the flame, Son of the light'.[34] He comes with a light that may seem foreign to us, and from which we may have cut ourselves off, but it is a light from the heart of life, not from beyond it. George MacDonald describes the incarnation of Christ as the coming of 'a real man' to those who are 'half-unreal', to show them the light that is hidden in the depths of life:

> Then God shone forth from all the lowly earth,
> And men began to read their maker there.[35]

Exercise

Meditating is a way of being aware of the light of God that is at the heart of life, and, in being aware, to be renewed in that light within ourselves.

Begin your meditation by finding the right position, whether that be seated with your feet on the floor or lying on your back or walking. There is no 'correct' position as such, apart from what is right for you. It is important, however, to have your back straight and to be alert within yourself.

In the Celtic tradition the practice of prayer often is pursued in the context of creation. If it is not possible for you to be outside, you may wish to meditate by an open window or in a space in which you can be aware of the elements of creation. The other possibility is to include a bowl of water, for instance, or plants or stones in your indoor place of prayer – symbols that can help make the connection between a prayerful awareness of God and the mystery of creation.

Begin to repeat silently the words derived from Psalm

43, 'Send out your light; let it bring me to your dwelling.' At the same time allow images and memories of light to be recalled within you.

It can be helpful to allow your breathing to set the rhythm of repetition. Try saying the words, 'Send out your light', as you breathe upwards. Feel your body expanding. Know that in prayer we are opening ourselves to the One who dwells at the heart of life. The light that we are seeking issues up from within. Then as you breathe downwards repeat the words, 'let it bring me to your dwelling'. Allow yourself to experience being led to the heart of light within you. Repeat these words meditatively for 15 minutes as you breathe in and out. Whenever distraction occurs, as it always does, simply return to the phrase as a way of focusing your inner attention.

After the 15 minutes of meditation, begin to express silently the prayers of your heart. What are the desires that God has planted in the depths of your being? Express these simply in prayer. Know that your deepest yearnings arise from the image of God within you. Allow them to awaken in you a sense of the longings for life and love that are in men and women throughout the world. For about five minutes pray for them as well. You may wish to complete your time of silence by saying the Lord's prayer or other closing words.

If you are meditating with others it can be helpful to share together some of what you have experienced in the silence. This is not a time for discussion but simply for listening to one another. Often it is in trying to give expression to our experiences of silence that we begin to comprehend what it was that was happening within us during mediation.

THE
SECOND DAY:
THE WILDNESS
OF GOD

2

The Second Day:
The Wildness of God

And God said, 'Let there be a dome in the midst of the waters, and let it separate the waters from the waters.' (Genesis 1:6)

The waters of Genesis 1 are interpreted by Eriugena as the dark mystery of God that enfolds all things. Into this essentially unknowable and infinite realm of God a dome of space and time is created. It is like a womb or matrix of life. In it will appear all that is to be created. St Paul speaks of the One 'in whom we live and move and have our being'.[1] Creation is planted, as it were, in the waters of God's life. It is rooted in the Unseen. All that is born in this matrix of life has its inception in the Infinite. Creation's life partakes of the essence of God's life, and to that extent is a theophany or manifestation of the mystery of God.

A mighty wind sweeps over the face of the waters.[2] Eriugena envisages this as a swirling movement of the four elements. Earth, air, fire and water, the constituents of everything that will be, are in a whirlwind of motion. It is a wild wind carrying the incipient life of the universe in its wings. If the 'first day' of creation is compared to the cosmic burst of light at life's initial moment, the 'second day' can be viewed as the ongoing explosion of elemental particles hurtling through space. There is nothing neat and tidy about this mighty creative energy. From it the matter of life emerges, as does lifeless matter, flung almost discardedly across space. Its power and expansiveness are overwhelming.

The Celtic tradition has a strong sense of the wildness of God. Like nature it is unrestrainable. A true worship of God, therefore, can neither be contained within the four walls of a sacred building nor restricted to the boundaries of religious tradition. The early Celtic Church was characterized by patterns of worship and prayer under the open skies. The high-standing crosses were gathering places and focal points of contemplation. Often they were situated in wild, exposed sites, as were the many Celtic monastic communities dotted along the coastlines of Ireland and Britain. Earth, sea and sky, rather than enclosed sanctuaries, were the temple of God. Small wooden churches and chapels were constructed by the Celtic mission, but the central and enduring symbols of its religious architecture point to the conviction that the holy mystery of God is unbounded.

This emphasis on worshipping in the context of nature can be traced with some confidence to pre-Christian religious practice in Britain. Few details are known of the Celtic nature mysticism that preceded Christianity for it was an oral tradition and left no written account of its beliefs and rituals. There were, however, sacred rivers and woods, many of which the Celtic Church baptized into its mission rather than rejecting. St Bride's sixth-century monastic community, for instance, was formed on the site of a holy oak grove. Its name 'Kildare' simply means 'the Church of the Oaks'. Contemporary Roman accounts refer to the pre-Christian holy men or 'druids' as living in 'deep groves' and 'solitary places'. With a note of astonishment they describe the druids as worshipping 'without making use of temples'.[3] It was typical of the Celtic Church to see its worship of Christ as building on the truths and symbols of the mysticism that had preceded Christianity in Britain. Aspects of its ancient mythology and nature religion were the equivalent of an Old Testament for the Celtic mission. Christ was the fulfilment of all that was true, whether that was of the priestly and prophetic traditions of Judaism or of its own Celtic druidical past.

Most of us will have vivid memories of the wildness of creation. Some of our first recollections from childhood will be of the strength of the waves of the sea, or of our faces being lashed with rain. A roaring fire under the open sky with the wind catching its flames high into the air makes a profound impression on us, and can release a sense of identification with the elements. So too can moments when we experience within ourselves a wild swirling of energies. Desires, emotions and creative urges suddenly surge up from our depths like whirlwinds. If channelled creatively they give rise to artistic expression, to action for justice, or to new birth in ourselves and relationships. Yet the wildness of these swirlings, whether from within or without, tend to be viewed predominantly as something we need to wrap up against or seek shelter from. In our religious traditions we have sought, almost exclusively, the gifts of peace and calm for our souls while neglecting to seek the inner stirrings of creative wildness.

George MacLeod writes of the Spirit moving upon 'the turbulent waters of our lives'.[4] Do we think that we can have creativity without such turbulence, whether that be creativity within ourselves or in our relationships or societies? The Book of Genesis portrays all things as born out of the wild wind that swept over the face of the waters. Are we expecting it to be entirely different in our lives? Do we think that creativity can emerge without surges of unordered energy rising from the unknown depths within us?

Part of what we fear, of course, is the uncontrollableness of wildness. We have witnessed it from afar in places of terrible violence in our world. We have experienced it in ourselves and in our relationships when the eruption of unexpected passion has led us along self-destructive paths. Have we thereby come to believe that wildness is essentially harmful, to be suppressed at all costs? What we need to reclaim is its creativity. At the beginning of life a mighty wind swept over the face of the deep. Creation emerges from this troubling of the waters. Yes, of course wildness can be destructive. We know that. But do we know also the wildness that is at the heart of creativity, like the passion that is at the beginning of life's conception? If we deny these depths of wildness the unsettled waters within us will turn to destructive rather than creative energy. Whether emotionally or sexually or artistically, when fear suppresses the energies in us that have their origin in the wildness of God, they will be turned into forces of death rather than vitality. Between us this leads to apathy or violence. Within us it means a dearth of creativity.

The Celtic tradition deeply affirms the unbounded side of life. It seeks a wild naturalness of place and an untameable energy of power. In the prayers of the Hebrides the elemental forces of earth, sea and sky are recognized as potentially destructive. The goodness of their wild energy, however, is invoked:

> Power of storm be thine,
> Power of moon be thine,
> Power of sun.
> Power of sea be thine,
> Power of land be thine,
> Power of heaven.[5]

Or as another blessing puts it:

> Thine be the might of river,
> Thine be the might of ocean, . . .
> The might of victory on field.
> Thine be the might of fire, . . .
> Thine be the might of element, . . .
> The might of the love on high.[6]

These are similar to the well-known lines of the famous 'Breastplate' hymn of St Patrick in which the strength of God is sought in the flashing of the lightning or in 'the whirling wind's tempestuous shocks'. The Celtic tradition reverences the power of elemental forces, while not being naive to their destructive potential. To be aware of creation's power and natural wildness is a grace that can help us recover the depths of wild creative energy that are within us as well.

The 'wind' in Genesis 1 is sometimes translated as 'the Spirit of God'. She is seen as a great bird brooding over the waters of chaos to bring creation to birth. Eriugena says that the Spirit 'fermented'[7] or 'fertilized the waters'.[8] These images convey a sense of life being drawn from the invisible into the visible. In its essence life is hidden in the mystery of God, but is drawn forth 'into visible forms and corporeal beauties'.[9]

In a meditation on this theme I saw dolphins leaping out of wild waters. They leapt with the synchronism that can characterize the movements of creatures through water and air. The image spoke of the emergence of the visible world out of the invisible waters of God. In the Celtic tradition it is not as if 'the dome in the midst of the waters' is entirely sealed off from the waters that surround it. The image is much more that of the waters of God's life being infused throughout the whole matrix of life. It is like a subterranean river running through all things. Although it is hidden and unseen, nothing has life apart from it.

George MacDonald, in his novel *Lilith*, imagines a land that has been so oppressed by evil that its waters have gone underground. They flow unseen, deep below the surface, unknown to the people and creatures of the land, but from these subterranean streams comes the moisture of life. The story in part is about the rediscovery of the great hidden river. It is sensed first by someone asleep on the ground, dreaming. He hears far beneath him the sound of many waters rushing over the stones of buried channels. It is, he says, a 'loveliest chaos of music-stuff'.[10] In the end the liberation of the submerged waters transforms the parched land into a garden of abundance.

This theme of the interweaving of God's life throughout all things is a primary characteristic of the Celtic tradition. George MacLeod speaks of 'the eternal seeping through the physical'.[11] Similarly he describes the veil that divides heaven from earth as 'thin as gossamer'.[12] A sense of 'thin-ness' between the material and spiritual realms, in which something of the eternal is glimpsed in and through the temporal, marks Celtic spirituality at every stage in its development. In the nineteenth century Alexander Scott describes creation as 'a transparency through which a light of God is seen'.[13] And Pelagius, at the beginnings of British Christianity, says that 'narrow shafts of divine light pierce the veil that separates heaven from earth'.[14] This is a spiri-tuality that looks not away from life to find God but deep within all that has life.

This interweaving of the spiritual and the material is conveyed in Celtic literature by stories, both Christian and pre-Christian in origin, of messengers from the other-world crossing back and forth into this world. Through a mist, or over the sea, suddenly a divine messenger will appear, whether in human or animal form or as a shape-shifting creature, to impart a sign or word of warning. As unexpectedly as its arrival it then disappears back into the mist or the sea. Celtic Christianity adapted this way of seeing into its own legends and stories. The pre-Christian festival of *Samhain*, for instance, which marked the beginning of the Celtic year on November 1, celebrated a lowering of barriers between the two worlds. Much of this was then incorporated by the Celtic mission into its celebration of All Saints on the same date, and the assurance of the closeness of heaven's company among us on earth.

Scant regard is paid in the Celtic tradition of story-telling to any strict sense of sequence in time and place. A freedom of imagination is used to weave together the whole of life, past and present, seen and unseen. Legends of St Bride, for instance, leap lightly back and forth between the birth of Christ in Palestine and the time of the flowering of Christianity in Ireland. The sixth-century Bride is portrayed as a barmaid in the Bethlehem inn, as well as midwife to Mary and wet-nurse to the Christ-child. Such a story conveys at levels deeper than historical congruity the union of heaven and earth in the mystery of Christ.

In the nineteenth century, George MacDonald can be seen applying this freedom of the imagination to the same end. Again there is the theme of the interweaving of the spiritual and the material. 'Ah, the two worlds! so strangely are they one', he writes, 'and yet so measurelessly wide apart!'[15] In his novel *Lilith*, he uses the image of a book that is, at one and the same time, in both worlds. On the shelves of a library in this world the book is only half present to those who do not know the other world. But in the hands of someone who sees spiritually, the book is present in both its parts and speaks of the marriage of heaven and earth. This is the Celtic tradition's approach to scripture and to the book of creation. They tell of the two worlds conjoined.

It is, perhaps above all else, in Celtic art that this theme is most powerfully conveyed. In what has come to be known as 'the everlasting pattern' in the Celtic tradition's beautiful illumination of Gospel manuscripts, or in its stone-carvings of high-standing crosses, the design is of inseparably interwoven strands. A human head at the end of one curve will become that of an animal or an angel at the end of the next. It all speaks of an interweaving of worlds, and of worlds within worlds. A delight is taken, even in the cross designs and Gospel illuminations, at the inclusion of wild animals amidst the flowing patterns. Always there is an awareness of the untameable and unpredictable. Through what are in fact strict methods of construction, using grids and compasses, an ungeometric and wild effect is achieved. Its patterns are ever-changing and hard to pin down. The essence of this art, in both its pre-Christian and Christian forms, is curvilinear design. The originality of the artist, like the creativity of the Creator, expresses itself not in straight-line patterns but in the free-flowing curves and swirling movements of nature.

The figure in the Celtic tradition who is connected most closely with the wildness of creation's elements is the Archangel Michael. He is regarded as patron saint of the sea and of horses. His name simply means 'One who resembles God'. As angel or messenger of God he is portrayed as riding an unbridled horse in the midst of the wind. The horse with no bit in his mouth is, according to Hebridean tradition,

> As white as the snow of the peaks,
> As white as the foam of the waves, . . .
> As swift as the wind of March, . . .
> As swift as the shaft of death.[16]

The horse and rider are elemental. They ride at the heart of the wind of God.

It was particularly at the great moments of transition in life, namely conception and death, that the aid of Michael was invoked. Women in barrenness and families in bereavement sought his help. These 'womb' and 'tomb' times represented a passing over from the invisible into the visible, or from the seen into the unseen. Similarly he was associated with the end of time when, in the midst of a mighty wind or cosmic fire, a new heaven and a new earth would be born.

Alexander Carmichael records some of the Hebridean customs in relation to the celebration of Michael each year on 29 September. This was considered a principal feast day in the Celtic calendar. It included a morning procession or 'circuiting' of the burial-ground on horseback, and later a wild racing of the horses, with neither saddle nor bridle, by both women and men. In preparation for the festivities it was permissible on the Eve of Michaelmas to steal a horse for use on the following day, with the understanding that it was to be returned after the Day of Michael. It was also a day of love-gifts and love-making, with promises and tokens of love exchanged between young men and women. Related to this was the giving and receiving of carrots as symbols of fertility and offspring. As a woman gathered her carrots in preparation for the festivities she would intone to herself words such as,

> Progeny on my womb, . . .
> Progeny on my progeny.[17]

And on the evening of Michaelmas, as part of the dance ritual, she would hold up her basket filled with carrots, and sing:

It is I myself that have the carrots,
Whoever he be that would win them from me.
It is I myself that have the treasure,
Whoso the hero could take them from me.[18]

Clearly these celebrations express the Celtic tradition's sense of the passion and wildness that are part of God's gifts of love and creativity. The 'stealing' of horses and the use of fertility symbols seem far removed from the order and decorum of much of our Western religious inheritance. They point, however, to a dimension of spirituality that for the most part we have lost sight of, the wildness of God.

The image of the Archangel Michael riding in the midst of the wind usually includes a flaming sword in his hand, and beneath him a dragon being slain. He rides not to subdue wildness but to subdue the dragon, a symbol of annihilation and destruction. The strength of passion or anger, like the strength of a storm, can be destructive. But Michael rides in the midst of the wind so that the stirrings of wildness, whatever they may be, can lead to life. We know the power for good or for evil that is in anger. The same can be said of any deep emotion or passion. Let us be clear that giving place to a wild energy from within ourselves is not about lawless self-will. It is not about doing whatever we please. Rather, it is about obeying a law planted deep in our nature, made as we are in the image of the One who is passionate. Just as Jesus was true to that dimension of himself in being angry at injustice in the temple and naming hypocrisy, or weeping passionately at the death of a friend, so in the service of love we may follow the wild energies that arise in us.[19]

A degree of wildness applied even to the way in which the ancient Celtic mission organized itself. It was not tightly controlled from one ecclesiastical centre, as in the Roman model. Rather, it consisted of a federation of monastic communities, with each monastery or family of monasteries enjoying considerable independence from the others. This gave rise to a variety in religious practice and to a lack of strict uniformity in liturgy, all of which in time irritated and threatened the centralized and highly uniform Roman mission. There was a type of family resemblance running through the Celtic tradition in Ireland and Britain but, like Celtic art, it was fluid rather than rigid. The unity came from within rather than being imposed from without.

One of the most striking features of this tradition was its love of wandering or peregrination. In its more extreme [*vision*] form, the *peregrini*, as they were called, would set sail in [*quest*] a boat without a rudder to be blown wherever the elements might take them. The ideal of the *peregrini* in the old Celtic Church was defined as 'seeking the place of one's resurrection'.[20] It consisted of a willingness to let go of or die to one's home, or the place that was comfortably familiar, in order to find new life. The impression given is that the gospel of Christ leads us not into what we already know but into what we do not yet know. George MacLeod, with reference to the Epiphany story of wise men from the East following the mysterious star of Christ, articulated a twentieth-century equivalent to peregrination when he said, 'Follow truth wherever you find it. Even if it takes you outside your preconceived ideas of God or life. Even if it takes you outside your own country into most insignificant alien places like Bethlehem.'[21]

In the Celtic tradition the search to find 'the place of one's resurrection' often led to the wildest and most elemental places. Remote islands and rocky outcrops were the Celtic equivalent to desert places of silence and prayer. The monastery of Skellig Michael is perhaps one of the most extreme and famous of these. It consisted of little more than a rock pinnacle eight miles off the coast of Kerry, Ireland. Its barrenness and isolation were suited to the Celtic tradition's stripped-down awareness of God in the elements. Centuries later, in the Hebrides, a common practice was to intone one's prayers along the wildness of a beach, allowing 'the voicing of the waves' and 'the praises of the ceaseless sea' to lead one into a sense of the presence of God.[22] In the twentieth century, Kenneth White put it in terms of being

> eager to get back out
> on to the naked shore
> there to walk for hours on end . . .
> trying to grasp at something
> that wanted no godly name
> something that took the form
> of blue waves and grey rocks
> and that tasted of salt[23]

The search is always for the Mystery that is deep within creation and yet infinitely other than anything we can know or name. It is a search that takes us into the wild and untamed places within ourselves as well as within nature.

In meditating on the mighty wind of the first chapter of Genesis one man saw the roof of his church being blown off. It is an image in keeping with the Celtic tradition. The wildness of the mystery of God is uncontainable. What we hear in the great book of creation may have a type of music about it, says White, but it is no 'easy harmonisation'. Rather, the wind and the sea with their 'unruled masses of sound' speak of 'a restlessness, a movingness' deep within creation.[24] This is what we hear in the book of scripture as well. The One who is the beginning and the end speaks in the mighty reverberations of 'seven thunders'.[25] Likewise the Son of Man, revealing truth with a two-edged sword in his mouth, is described in elemental terms. 'His eyes were like a flame of fire,' writes St John the Divine, 'his voice was like the sound of many waters . . . and his face was like the sun shining with full force.'[26] At the heart of the Celtic tradition is a reverencing of Christ as 'Son of the elements'.[27] In his body and blood is the wildness of God. With a passion of love he comes 'to bring fire to the earth'.[28]

Exercise

Meditating is a way of being reconnected to the creativity that is deep within us.

Begin your time of meditation by finding the right position and the right place, preferably a place in which you are not likely to be interrupted. As Jesus says, 'Whenever you pray, go into your room and shut the door and pray to your Father who is in secret; and your Father who sees in secret will reward you.'[29] Meditation is a time of shutting the doors of our minds to distraction in order to be more deeply alert.

Repeat silently the words from Psalm 104, 'You ride on the wings of the wind'. At the same time allow images and memories of wind and wildness to be recalled within you.

If you wish to use your breathing to set the rhythm of repetition, try saying the words 'You ride on the wings of the wind' as you breathe downwards. Allow this to remind you that in prayer you are addressing the One who dwells at the heart of your life and of all life. Then as you breathe upwards and feel your body expanding, be aware of the creative energies that you are opening up to from the depths of your being. Repeat the words meditatively for 15 minutes as a way of being renewed in those depths.

After the 15 minutes of meditation, begin to express silently the prayers of your heart. Allow your own heart's desires to link you with the yearnings for new beginnings and creativity that are deep within people throughout the world. Pray for them as well. After about five minutes of silent prayer close with the Lord's prayer or other words.

If you are meditating with others, share together some of what you have experienced in the silence. This is a time for listening to one another and for reflecting on what you have heard.

THE THIRD DAY: THE FECUNDITY OF GOD

3

The Third Day:
The Fecundity of God

And God said, 'Let the waters under the sky be gathered into one place, and let the dry land appear.' And it was so. God called the dry land Earth, and the waters that were gathered together he called Seas. And God saw that it was good. (Genesis 1:9–10)

Out of the elemental swirl of the second day there now emerges what Eriugena calls 'the most beautiful firmness' of the earth.[1] If the second day points to the wild creativity of God in the vast expanses of space, the third day portrays God fashioning the earth in stability and fruitfulness. Fertile land appears out of the fermentation of the waters and brings forth vegetation, 'plants yielding seed', says Genesis, and 'trees of every kind bearing fruit'.[2] They are 'nourished and fattened', writes Eriugena, by the moisture that is in the earth.[3] The picture is of the fecundity of life.

St John says that 'in the beginning was the Word, and the Word was with God, and the Word was God'.[4] He also says that all things have come into being through the Word. Standing in the mystical tradition of St John, the Celtic tradition teaches that creation is essentially an utterance of God. It is spoken forth from 'the secret recesses of the Father's substance'. It is, says Eriugena, 'always being born'.[5] In the nineteenth century Alexander Scott further developed this perspective by describing creation as the child of God. All things at heart are a birth or embodiment of God's Word. This is not to say that everything that we see or hear in creation is a perfect expression of God. We know that life is streaked through with all sorts of distortion and suffering. At the beginning or centre of life, however, is the Word. God utters creation forth from the heart of the universe.

St John describes Christ as the Word 'made flesh'.[6] Christ is in that sense the perfect expression of God. He truly reveals the Word that is at the beginning of all things. 'The whole lesson of creation', says Scott, 'is gathered up in Christ.'[7] As the Spirit conceives of the Christ-child in the waters of Mary's womb, so creation is born of the Spirit in the virgin womb of the universe. Christ reveals the essential truth of the cosmos. It is born of God.

The Genesis account makes special mention of the seeds that are planted in the earth, 'plants yielding seed of every kind' and 'fruit with the seed in it'.[8] Eriugena refers to this as 'the seminal force' that is hidden within the earth.[9] The profusion of plants and trees that issue from the ground is a manifestation of this seed force. Their roots reach down to the earth's 'concealed depths' for the waters that sustain them.[10] The moisture that is within the soil of the earth is for Eriugena a symbol of the waters of God that enfold and infuse all things. Everything that is born in the great matrix of life is sustained by roots that reach into the deep mystery of God's life.

An Irish priest, in meditating on the third day of creation, recollected from his boyhood the fresh springs of water that surged up from beneath the fields of his family farm. Not only did these sustain the crops, they were the source of his family's water supply. His memories were of working hard and sweating in the fields, and of plunging his head into the pools to drink deeply of pure, cool, spring water. This is an image of the goodness that wells up from within life.

The Genesis account says, 'And God saw that it was good'. Eriugena speaks of 'the ineffable fertility of the Divine Goodness'.[11] Elsewhere he calls it the 'fecundity' of God.[12] Kenneth White's way of putting it is to say:

I have grown chrysanthemums in the dung of God[13]

It all speaks not only of the sheer abundance of the earth's fertility, but also of the essential goodness of what grows from the ground. The Celtic tradition is led to affirm that the goodness of God is at the very heart and inception of all life. 'The Divine Goodness', as Eriugena says, 'summons all things out of not-being into being.'[14] This is not to be naive to the ways in which creation is blighted and diseased. The people of the Celtic fringe of Britain and Ireland have not been strangers to famine and natural hardship. Despite this the Celtic tradition has celebrated the goodness that is deeper than evil.

So essential is goodness to creation that Eriugena saw that, if goodness were to be entirely removed from life, nothing would remain. 'Goodness', he says, 'does not come through essence but essence comes through goodness.'[15] In other words, it is not that goodness is merely a characteristic of life. Rather, it is the very source of life. 'For all things that are,' he says, 'are in so far as they are good, but in so far as they are not good, or rather, in so far as they are less good, to that extent they are not.'[16] The Celtic tradition thus proceeds to define evil as essentially destructive. 'As goodness conducts existing things out of non-existence in order that they may be, so wickedness strives to corrupt all things that are and to dissolve them utterly so that they may not be.'[17] The momentum of evil is always towards non-being and meaninglessness. The degree to which any created thing becomes evil is the extent to which it ceases to truly exist. It becomes false to itself.

To experience the goodness in life, therefore, is to be in touch with the gift of God. We all have memories of the goodness of creation. We have smelled the freshness of the earth after rain. We have known the delight of biting into a crisp autumn apple. We have gazed upon field after field of golden corn. We have touched the cool smoothness of a rock, sea-washed for millennia. The goodness is there. We are called into an awareness of it, to be alert, as Alexander Scott taught, to 'the fathomless mystery involved in the mere existence of a pebble'.[18]

George MacDonald, long anticipating some of the ecological awarenesses of the twentieth century, described the grandmother figure in his novel, *The Golden Key*, as at one with the mystery of creation. Typically, MacDonald uses a wise and beautiful old woman to represent the divine. Clad in a green dress, she lives in a great wood and is always barefooted. Those who visit her similarly are invited to take off their shoes. To touch the ground with their bare feet is to become more alive to the vibrancy of the goodness that is in the earth. The allusion is clearly to the Book of Exodus and the story of Moses encountering God in the flames of a blazing bush. 'Remove the sandals from your feet,' says God, 'for the place on which you are standing is holy ground.'[19] In the Celtic tradition all ground is holy, for within it is the goodness of God.

We all know what a difference it can make to be barefooted. To feel the soft moisture of grass beneath our feet opens new awarenesses in us. It can allow us to see life with a different perspective. The same, of course, can be said about walking on rough terrain. To expose our feet to stony ground also leads to new awarenesses! A heightened sense of the earth on which we walk is not just about pleasurable experiences. It is about knowing and reverencing the creation of which we are a part. Gerard Manley Hopkins, whose years in the Celtic culture of northern Wales inspired much of his poetry, writes of the way in which we have cut ourselves off from feeling the grandeur of God in creation. By 'being shod', he says, our feet can no longer feel. We have lost touch with 'the dearest freshness deep down things'.[20]

The answer to our extreme insensitivities to creation in the Western world today does not lie in a resumed practice of going barefooted. We need to find new ways of re-opening the doors of our senses to creation, whether we live in crowded cities or open countryside. The experience of feeling the earth with our feet is a symbol of the rediscovery that needs to happen if we are to come back into a true sense of relationship with creation. This can happen through an attentiveness to the mystery of what grows in our city gardens and household plant pots, as it will happen also in the vast stretches of open fields of the country and in our ancient woods. It is the experience of the goodness of the earth that will help sustain our commitment to care for the earth.

The practice of going barefooted, of course, is still common in other parts of the world. During my time at the Benedictine monastery of Shantivanam in Tamil Nadu, India, I was struck by the number of occasions in which it was expected that we should walk barefooted. In meditation at sunrise along the banks of the holy river Cauvary we would walk with bare feet, feeling the morning coolness of the path beneath us.

Similarly at prayer in the Christian temple, or in visiting Hindu temples, we would take off our shoes on entering. And in eating together, seated on the floor of the monastery's refectory, again we would be barefooted as a way

of showing reverence for one another and for the gifts of
the earth.

Because India was a place in which so often shoes were
not worn, I particularly noticed the occasions on which I
kept mine on firmly. I, for instance, did not go barefooted
in visiting a leper colony or a hospice for the dying. And
my experience one night on an unlit side-street in Madras
is one that I shall for ever feel ashamed of. I stumbled over
a shape that seemed no larger than a young child. When
I looked more closely at what my foot had caught, I saw
that it was a little old woman. She was curled up for the
night, with a sack to cover her. My reaction was to hurry
along, feeling slightly relieved that I had not touched her
with bare feet. What is it in us that so often wants to cover
over our sensitivities, to both the glory and the pain? Is it
not that such sensitivity will challenge us in our lifestyles
and in our relationships with one another and the earth?

What are we to do with our perception of God's goodness in the earth, and in the gifts and people of the earth?
In part it is given that we may see such goodness as a
theophany of God, a showing forth of the One whose
beauty and fecundity are within life as well as immeasur-
ably beyond it. But how is it to affect the way we live,
both individually and collectively?

This is where the Celtic insistence on the relationship
between nature and grace is so important. At the very
beginning of the tradition, Pelagius had pointed to what
he called 'the good of nature and the good of grace'.[21] Both
are gifts of God. Would we, he asks, think of saying that
'the glowing lights of the moon or the stars serve the rich
man more than the poor'?[22] Every 'good gift', says St
James, is of God.[23] Have the gifts of nature been given
more for one type of person than for another? Would we
think of saying that the gifts of the altar are exclusively

for the rich, or that better wine and better bread are to be
given to some and not to others? And yet, says Pelagius,
this is exactly what we have done with God's gift of nature:

> Does it seem just to you then that one man should have
> an abundance of riches over and above his needs, while
> another does not have enough even to supply his daily
> wants? That one man should relax in the enjoyment of
> his wealth, while another wastes away in poverty? That
> one man should be full to bursting-point with expensive
> and sumptuous banquets far in excess of nature's
> habitual requirements, while another has not even
> enough cheap food to satisfy him. That one should pos-
> sess a vast number of splendid houses adorned with
> costly marble statues in keeping with the instincts of his
> vanity and pride, while another has not even a tiny hovel
> to call his own and to protect him from the cold or the
> heat? That one man should maintain countless pos-
> sessions and enormous expanses of land, while another
> cannot enjoy the possession even of a small portion of
> turf on which to sit down? That one man should be rich
> in gold, silver, precious stones and all kinds of material
> possessions, while another is harassed by hunger, thirst,
> nakedness and all kinds of poverty?[24]

God's generosity to humankind, he said, is given for all
people, both through the gift of nature and the gift of
grace. Any inequality in the dispensation of these gifts is
due not to God but to human injustice. 'For why would
God want men to be unequal in the lesser things', asked
Pelagius, 'when he has made them equal in the greater?'[25]

This was a formative stage in the development of the
Celtic tradition's emphasis on grace and nature. It saw that
the goodness of the gift of nature is to be distributed
equally. To not do so would be the same as refusing to

share the gift of grace. At this point Pelagius came into further conflict with Augustine, for the latter was teaching a doctrine of predestination that limited the grace of God. Only some were chosen by God to receive the grace of salvation. The rest of humanity was to be judged for its essentially sinful nature. This same conflict was to appear again and again over the centuries between the Celtic tradition and the Roman. Eriugena was criticized for his opposition to a belief in predestination, as was Alexander Scott in the nineteenth century. He and others were deposed from the ministry because of their insistence that the grace of God is not to be limited. The Celtic tradition has consistently refused to place tight boundaries on the generosity of God's giving, whether that be of grace or of nature. The very rising of the sun each morning is a gift of God, given for the whole of creation, no less than the gift of redemption, given to restore creation to its essential well-being.

In relation to the goodness of the earth's resources, Pelagius taught that there are three types of people: those who have enough, those who have not enough, and those who have more than enough. 'Let no man have more than he really needs', he said, 'and everyone will have as much as they need, since the few who are rich are the reason for the many who are poor.'[26] Pelagius taught a type of redistribution of the gifts of nature. 'All should possess impartially', he said, 'and with equal rights.'[27]

Although it cannot be proved that Pelagius's emphasis on a just distribution of the earth's resources contributed to the eventual papal excommunication and imperial ban against him, one wonders what part it played in the judgement. Similarly, and on a larger scale in seventh-century Britain, what effect did the Celtic tradition's commitment to simplicity have on the outcome of the decisive Synod of

Whitby? The Celtic mission's practice of sharing its gifts with the poor rather than amassing wealth for itself stood in sharp contrast to the increasingly rich and powerful Roman mission. This is not to say that Celtic monasticism had a monopoly on charity. But its legends of great saints like Bride and others giving away their possessions, and sometimes even giving away what was not theirs, reflects the cherished place of generosity in the Celtic tradition.

As Christians, said Pelagius, we are to live by 'Christ's example', imparting to others what we most desire for ourselves.[28] He appeals again and again in his writings to Christ's teaching from Matthew's Gospel, 'In everything do to others as you would have them do to you; for this is the law and the prophets.'[29] This, for Pelagius, is the epitome of gospel righteousness. 'You should pick out and inscribe over your heart this sentence of the gospel,' he says. 'For whenever you have the kind of attitude to another that you wish another to maintain towards you, then you are keeping to the way of righteousness; but whenever you are the kind of person to another that you want no one to be to you, you have abandoned the way of righteousness.'[30]

Goodness, then, is not simply defined in terms of refraining from evil but of actively doing good, and thereby participating in the generosity of God:

> Indeed, you are instructed not only not to strip one who is clothed of his garments but also to cover one who has been stripped of his garments with your own; nor only not to take bread away from one who has it but willingly to bestow your own on one who has none; nor only not to drive a poor man out of his lodging but also to receive into your own one who has been driven out of his and has none as a result.[31]

Putting the stress on positive acts of goodness rather than merely a cautious observance of restraining from evil, Pelagius refers to Matthew 25 and its theme of judgement upon those who have not fed the hungry, welcomed the stranger or clothed the naked. The condemnation in the gospel story, he says, is based not on whether they have done evil by committing adultery, theft or murder, for example, but on whether they have done good.

The practice of hospitality is particularly encouraged in the Celtic tradition. Pelagius defines the Christian as one 'whose door is closed to no one' and 'whose food is offered to all'.[32] Centuries later in the Western Isles of Scotland there was a further development of this emphasis, in relation to the identification of Christ with the homeless and the poor. To be committed to welcoming unknown travellers into one's house, and sharing food and drink with them, was to be open to being visited by Christ himself. The Iona Community of today still uses the ancient rune of hospitality from the Hebrides in welcoming its guests to the Abbey each week:

> We saw a stranger yesterday,
> We put food in the eating place,
> drink in the drinking place,
> music in the listening place,
> and with the sacred name of the Triune God,
> he blessed us and our house,
> our cattle and our dear ones.
> As the lark says in her song,
> Often, often, often goes Christ in the stranger's
>   guise.[33]

Other Hebridean prayers seek 'Plenty of food, plenty of drink, plenty of beds, and plenty of ale' for the house and the table that are open to all.[34] The essential place of generosity in the Christian life had been underlined by Pelagius at the very beginnings of Celtic Christianity when he asked, 'Do you consider a man to be a Christian by whose bread no hungry man is ever filled, by whose drink no thirsty man is refreshed, whose table no one knows, [and] beneath whose roof neither stranger nor traveller comes at any time?'[35]

Pelagius's emphasis on sharing the goodness of the earth may have been addressed primarily to individuals rather than to society as a whole, but later in the Celtic tradition the corporate and political dimensions were added. Alexander Scott, for instance, was one of the founders of Christian Socialism. This was a daring attempt in mid nineteenth-century Britain to call for a re-ordering of society on the basis of cooperative principles. Scott criticized those who dominated the wealth and natural resources of the country, and who argued against political change on the basis of a divinely instituted hierarchy of power and privilege. 'God is the God of order', agreed Scott, 'but not necessarily pledged to that particular form of order, by which your quiet and your wealth seem to you to be best secured.'[36] Those who consider that the Celtic tradition is merely a romanticized nature-mysticism need to hear the hard-hitting words of Celtic teachers again and again over the centuries. To claim that both nature and grace are gifts of God given for all is to offer a spirituality that engages deeply with the life of the world and that calls emphatically for a just distribution of the earth's resources.

Alongside the Celtic belief in the essential goodness of creation is the conviction that we are part of that goodness. We are like fields, says Pelagius, with the fertility of God's life within us. Here, too, 'crops' of goodness are to be reaped and shared.[37] The fallow fields of our souls that have been 'long left unploughed' need to be turned over. Then we will see that deeper than any fallowness in us is the fecundity of God.

Exercise

Meditating is a way of becoming aware of the rich depths of God's goodness within us.

Begin your time of meditation by finding the right position and the right place, whether that be inside or out of doors. Be intentional about choosing or creating the space that will be most conducive to meditating on both scripture and creation.

Repeat silently the words derived from Psalm 33, 'The earth is full of your goodness'. At the same time allow images and memories of the goodness of the earth to be recalled within you.

If you wish to use your breathing to set the rhythm of repetition, try saying the words, 'The earth is full of your goodness', as you breathe downwards. Allow this to remind you that in prayer you are addressing the One who dwells at the heart of life. Then as you breathe upwards and feel your body expanding, be aware of the goodness that you are opening up to from the depths of your being. It is planted within you and can be sensed like the fragrance of the earth's goodness. Repeat the words meditatively for 15 minutes.

After 15 minutes of meditation, begin to express silently the prayers of your heart. Allow your own heart's desires to link you with the longings for life and goodness that are within men and women everywhere. Pray for them as well. After about five minutes of silent prayer close with the Lord's prayer or other words.

If you are meditating with others, share together some of what you have experienced in the silence. This is a time for listening and for reflecting on what you have heard within yourself and in one another.

THE
FOURTH DAY :
THE HARMONY
OF GOD

4

The Fourth Day:
The Harmony of God

*And God said, 'Let there be lights in the dome of
the sky ... to give light upon the earth.' And it
was so. God made the two great lights – the greater
light to rule the day and the lesser light to rule the
night – and the stars.* (Genesis 1:14–16)

The unbridled wind of God's creativity gives birth not only
to the 'beautiful firmness' of the earth on the third day but
now to the lights of the skies, or to what Eriugena calls
the 'celestial luminaries'.[1] The sun, moon and stars, in their
harmonies of movement and light, are further theophanies
or showings of God. Shining out of the darkness of space
they express something of the inexpressible. 'There is no
speech, nor are there words,' says the Psalmist, 'yet their
voice goes out through all the earth.'[2] The sun by day and
the moon by night declare the mystery of God. What is it
that they are saying?

Eriugena reminds us that the nature of God is essentially
unknowable 'since the Inaccessible Light transcends every
intellect'.[3] The great luminaries of the sky, however, are
born of the 'Father of lights'.[4] Through them 'God is
expressing himself', says Scott.[5] As one of the characters
in Kenneth White's poem, 'The Eight Eccentrics', says,

> When people ask me to explain the way
> I just point to the sun and the moon.[6]

Like all that has been created, they are utterances of the
Word. To not listen to them is to ignore the self-disclosure
of God.

The Celtic tradition has been characterized over the centuries by a great awareness of the heavenly bodies. In the
Western Isles there was the belief that a love of the lights
of the skies, like a love of any aspect of creation, brought
with it a type of grace from God. The mystery at the heart
of creation is Love. To be in love with the gift of nature
is to be well within oneself. Invocation blessings in the
Carmina Gadelica tradition sought the grace of well-being
that accompanies a reverencing of creation:

> Grace of the love of the skies be thine,
> Grace of the love of the stars be thine,
> Grace of the love of the moon be thine,
> Grace of the love of the sun be thine.[7]

The Hebridean awareness of the skies partly grew out of
the crofting and seafaring nature of life in the islands. The
light of the sun by day gave growth to the crops in the
fields, and a moonlit night safely guided fishermen home
through dark seas and around dangerous reefs. The moon
was thus referred to with great affection. But this was
more than simply an appreciative awareness of the sun
and moon. It was also a reverencing of the light that is in
them.

Until well into the nineteenth century it was common
practice in parts of the Western Isles for people to venerate
the lights of the sky at the beginning of the day and at
night. As a woman from Barra recounted to Carmichael:

In time of my father and of my mother there was no

man in Barra who would not take off his bonnet to the
white sun of power, nor a woman in Barra who would
not bend her body to the white moon of the seasons.
No, my dear, not a man nor woman in Barra. And old
persons will be doing this still, and I will be doing it
myself sometimes.[8]

By late in the nineteenth century, there was considerable
opposition to the ancient prayers and customs of the Celtic
tradition. In Scotland the rigid Calvinism of the day was
declaring these practices to be pagan and pre-Christian.
They may well have had a pre-Christian influence. The
reverencing of the sun and the moon that was being
repressed, however, was explicitly Christian. These acts
were accompanied by making the sign of the cross. In
Celtic art, of course, the design of the cross incorporates
a sun symbol into its very structure. The sun at the centre
is held in the arms of the cross. This was not nature worship. It was a Christ-mysticism that reverenced nature. Like
St Paul's vision of all things, both visible and invisible,
being held together in Christ, it saw spiritual light and
physical light as interwoven.[9] And yet the fear of this mysticism and the repression of it grew until, by Carmichael's
time, a reverencing of the sun and moon was being visibly
practised only here and there in the Hebrides. So oppressive
was the opposition by parish ministers and schoolmasters
that Carmichael found the people reluctant to impart to
him the prayers and hymns of their tradition, for fear of
persecution.

Carmichael, however, did manage to transcribe many of
the sun and moon prayers. The following is one that was
used, normally by men, either at the rising of the sun over
the mountain peaks to the east or at its setting into the
western sea:

The eye of the great God,
The eye of the God of glory,
The eye of the King of hosts,
The eye of the King of the living,
Pouring upon us
At each time and season,
Pouring upon us
Gently and generously.
Glory to thee,
Thou glorious sun.
Glory to thee, thou sun,
Face of the God of life.[10]

The moon, which was reverenced as the 'great lamp of grace' because of its powers of guidance and influence, was similarly addressed, usually by women:

Hail to thee, thou new moon,
Guiding jewel of gentleness!
I am bending to thee my knee,
I am offering thee my love.

I am bending to thee my knee,
I am giving thee my hand,
I am lifting to thee mine eye,
O new moon of the seasons.

Hail to thee, thou new moon,
Joyful maiden of my love!
Hail to thee, thou new moon,
Joyful maiden of the graces!

Thou art travelling in thy course,
Thou art steering the full tides;
Thou art illuming to us thy face,
O new moon of the seasons.

Thou queen-maiden of guidance,
Thou queen-maiden of good fortune,
Thou queen-maiden my beloved,
Thou new moon of the seasons![11]

Both the sun and the moon were regarded as messengers of grace, as the following blessing from the *Carmina Gadelica* makes clear. They were placed in the same company as saints and angels:

The love and affection of heaven be to you,
The love and affection of the saints be to you,
The love and affection of the angels be to you,
The love and affection of the sun be to you,
The love and affection of the moon be to you,
Each day and night of your lives.[12]

We may feel distant from much of this. At another level, however, some of our deepest experiences of the mystery of light will resonate with the reverent awareness of the sun and moon in this tradition. We know what it is like to see the brilliance of the morning sun emerge out of the darkness of night to awaken the earth. We have felt on our faces and bodies the sun's revitalizing energy at times of exhaustion and weakness. Similarly we have known, sometimes in ways that render us speechless, the power of the moon to convey a sense of the mystery of creation.

The difference between our lives in the twentieth-century Western world and the lives of these men and women in the Celtic tradition of the past is that generally we have fallen out of a conscious relationship with the gift of the lights of the skies. It is not that we have no experience of their wonder. Nearly all of us can remember, even if it is only from the earliest memories of childhood, gazing into the infinity of the night sky and its countless spectrum of stars. What we have lost is a sense of rhythm and occasion for naming such moments. The challenge is to find new ways of naming these experiences so that our awareness is kept alive. We will then desire patterns of living that keep us in relationship to the lights of the sun and moon, and thus to the light of God.

It is no coincidence that it was men who took off their cap to the sun in the morning and women who bent their knee to the moon at night. In the Celtic tradition the light of the sun was viewed in masculine terms, just as the moon's light was seen as feminine. The associations of the sun's brilliance of strength were with power and outward energy. It was identified with clarity, with seeing things by the light of day, and thus with reason and intellect.

The light of the moon, on the other hand, was seen as soft and gentle. In the *Carmina Gadelica* tradition it was identified with the intuitive and with the flow of feeling and emotion:

> May the moon of moons
> Be coming through thick clouds
> On me and on every one
> Coming through dark tears.[13]

It had associations with the sensual, with the rhythm of the seasons, the ebb and flow of the tides, and with the menstrual cycle of women.

The light of the moon does not banish the dark as the sun does, flooding the world with its light. Rather, the moon is like a lamp in the night. It knows the night rather than fearing it. Darkness is allowed its space, and mystery is revealed. As the *Carmina Gadelica* says,

> Holy be each thing
> Which she illumines.[14]

This is not to say that the light of the moon makes each thing holy, but rather that in her light the holiness of each thing is more readily perceived. It is a quality of light which, in our urbanized contexts and ways of life, we often have lost contact with. We need to rediscover ways of experiencing the light of the night, for it can open in us perceptions that are complementary to seeing by the light of day.

In the Celtic tradition the sun is a masculine theophany of God and the moon a feminine theophany. What happens when we lose one of these, or allow the one to obscure the other? In a meditation on the fourth day of Genesis, one woman saw the moon fall from the sky. She then saw within herself the execution of a woman prisoner that was to take place in America the following day. These images speak of the demise of the feminine and of the displacement of feminine qualities of compassion in the shaping of justice and the ordering of our lives, both corporately and individually.

It would not be right to give the impression that the Celtic tradition has perfectly held in balance the masculine and feminine theophanies of God. The great weight of cultural norms in the Western world, and the patriarchal imagery that dominates scripture, led Celtic Christianity, like the rest of the Church, towards a masculine bias in divine imagery. There has always been, however, a significant desire and tendency in the Celtic tradition to use more than masculine imagery to point to the mystery of God.

We have noted all along the Celtic insistence on preserving a sense of the mystery and essential unknowableness of God. Any image of the Mystery, whether male or female, is set in perspective by affirming that God is more and other than anything that we can know or imagine. Eriugena described this as based on two ways of knowing, the *via positiva* and the *via negativa*. The negative way of knowing, which has always been cherished within mystical traditions, is to say that God is not this and God is not that. 'The Image of God', he said, 'is neither male nor female.'[15] This is in line with St Paul's emphasis in Galatians, when he says that in Christ there is 'neither male nor female'.[16]

The positive way of knowing, on the other hand, affirms that there is in God both the masculine and the feminine. There is a mother's heart at the heart of God, as well as a father's. The prophet Isaiah compares God's love to a mother's when he asks, 'Can a woman forget her nursing child, or show no compassion for the child of her womb?'[17] Similarly Malachi, using the image of fatherhood, asks, 'Have we not all one father? Has not one God created us?'[18] In essence God is neither male nor female, but in his theophanies God is both. And so it is to both that we may look in our search to know more of the Unknowable.

To speak of the mystery of God's life is to speak also of the mystery of our lives, for we are made in the image of God. The essence of who we are, therefore, is neither masculine nor feminine. At heart we are an unfathomable mystery, deeper than any such categories. And yet there are manifestations from within us of both the masculine and the feminine. Our inner world is a microcosm of the outer. We know within ourselves a combination of lights. There is intellect and intuition, for instance, just as there is reason as well as feeling. But the pressure in our Western inheritance has been to be one or the other. Change is coming, but as a man often I have been expected to live almost exclusively out of the masculine dimension of who I am. This has robbed us at times of knowing the other dimensions of who we are. It has led also to a dearth of resources today in exploring issues of sexual identity. We have been predisposed as a tradition against men who show their feminine depths, and feel threatened by women who have strong masculine energies.

The Celtic tradition celebrates the marriage of the two, both within ourselves and in relationship. It encourages a discovery of the hidden depths of who we are and an integration of these with what we already know. To discover gentleness and mystery within ourselves, for example, is not to abandon our strength and clarity of reasoning. George MacDonald, in exploring this theme in one of his short stories, sees such an integration as part of our redemption. Describing a redemptive change that has come upon a family, he writes, 'The voices of the men were deeper, and yet seemed by their very depth more feminine than before.'[19] Wholeness is a harmony of the masculine and the feminine. It is 'the heart in the head, the head in the heart, the equipoise of the soul', as Alexander Scott said.[20]

The Celtic tradition sees Christ as the beginning of this 'unification'. He shows us 'an example of the restoration of human nature', says Eriugena.[21] To be truly human is to be integrated with what is deepest within us. Christ directs us towards 'the experience of this harmony', says Scott.[22] We can know within ourselves when we are being reintegrated with the depths of what God has planted within us. It is like the harmony of what God has placed in the heavens. As the *Carmina Gadelica* says, Christ is both 'Son of the moon' and 'Son of the sun'.[23] He reveals to us the law of our being, which is the same as the law of the sun and the moon moving in a harmony of relationship. To conform to this law is to be set free.

The old Celtic Church displayed something of this integration in its life and mission. Double monasteries, for instance, were not untypical of the way it organized itself. These were religious communities of men and women pursuing their lives of monastic discipline together. Significant numbers of these were headed up by women – Bride of Kildare and Hilda of Whitby being two of the most well known. This is not to pretend that at times there were not difficulties in such a system. Life at the double monastery of Coldingham in the seventh century, for instance, seems not always to have been conducive to the fulfilling of monastic vows! The strength of the Celtic tradition on this matter, however, as in its practice of clerical marriage, was to see the essential goodness of masculine and feminine attraction and to make room for it in a variety of ways, rather than primarily fearing it and shutting it out.

The Celtic Church had received from its pre-Christian cultural inheritance certain patterns of integration that were baptized into its life. The ancient Celtic tradition of women warriors, for instance, provided a model of the feminine that helped free women from being seen exclusively in gentle and domestic terms. Similarly, Irish mythology offered a sense not only of the beauty of the feminine but of its dignity. Many of the ancient myths of love-making and marriage between god and goddess conveyed wonderfully rich images of equality and witty interplay between the feminine and masculine.

Likewise, the pre-Christian calendar of feast days, with its recurring theme of fertility, provided imagery of the relationship between masculine and feminine in creation. The spring festival of Beltane, for instance, on the first of May – a tradition that continued into Celtic Christianity – celebrated the waxing power of the sun being responded to by the fecundity of the earth. The sun's life-giving force was symbolized by the lighting of fires, accompanied by music and dance. It marked the beginnings of the summer grazing on the hillsides.

George MacDonald's fairy-tale, 'Little Daylight', is the story of a young princess who falls under the curse of an evil fairy who banishes her from the sun. The effect of the curse is that she will sleep all day and wake at night, and that her feminine beauty will wax and wane with the light of the moon. In part this is a story of the way in which evil distances us from dimensions of who we most truly are. The princess's name is Daylight, her hair is golden like the sun, and her eyes are as blue as the sky on a clear day, and yet she lives as a fugitive from the day.

Into the fairy-tale comes the prince, whose kiss will release the princess from her curse and banishment. His love for her draws him further and further into an acquaintance with the night and its moonlight. At first he is confused by the night's light and stumbles in the forest. Eventually, however, he finds the princess. She is in an open glade in the midst of the wood, dancing and singing under the fullness of the moon. It is their kiss that frees them. Love has drawn the prince from the day into the night and has set the princess free from her captivity to the night to live also in the day. This is a story about finding our well-being in the coming together of the masculine and feminine, both within ourselves and in relationship.

Eriugena says that God is the beauty that is within everything that has been created, and that 'His beauty draws all things to Himself'.[24] He also says that the nature of God is love, and that this Love wills to be loved by all. Deep within us is a yearning for God, whether we become conscious of it 'under the guidance of grace' or whether it is by 'the simple appetite of nature'. At the heart of who we are is a longing for Love, 'for there is nothing that has been created by it that does not have desire for it'.[25]

Part of this desire is the attraction between the feminine and the masculine dimensions of the image of God within us and within one another. The 'original appetite of the human soul', as Scott calls it, 'may get confused ... but we are not therefore to deny its existence, nor to refuse the wholesome satisfaction of its demands'.[26] Our confusions lead us astray into all sorts of mirages of what will fulfil our desires. The answer is not to suppress the longings that arise from deep within us but to know where our true longings come from and what it is that will satisfy them.

Of course, there are false cravings and fantasies within us, sexual and otherwise, but do we know the goodness of the desires for life and love that are planted at the core of our being? Kenneth White speaks of 'knowing things in the deep pleasure-core'.[27] To be satisfied at that level is to be freed from the confusions that assail us in the other dimensions of who we are.

In Scotland the meeting of the day with the night is called the 'gloaming'. Old tales speak of it as a time when lovers meet. In Celtic legend the twilight, or the period of the 'two-lights', is a mystical time when an encounter between the visible world and the invisible world is more likely to occur. Birdsong announces the time of the two lights even when we are unaware of it. Kenneth White writes:

> sometimes in certain lights
> I think I have it
> (that last glance over the coast rocks
> in the gathering evening ...
> or in the white mist of early morning)
> but there's no exactitude[28]

It is the transitional moment of seeing that is neither the day's nor the night's but the merging of the two. It is the

marriage of the time of the sun with the time of the moon.
It is a theophany of the harmony of God.

Exercise

Meditating is a way of being reunited to the harmony of
God that is deep within life.

Begin your time of meditation by finding the right position and the right place, whether that be inside or out of
doors. Be intentional about choosing or creating the space
that is most conducive to meditating on both scripture and
creation.

Repeat silently the words derived from Job 38, 'You give
birth to the lights of the skies'. At the same time allow
images and memories of the sun, moon and stars to be
recalled within you.

If you wish to use your breathing to set the rhythm of
repetition, try saying the words, 'You give birth to the
lights of the skies', as you breathe upwards. Feel your body
expanding. Know that God has filled the universe with
lights, and that they have come to birth from the light that
is at the heart of life. Then as you breathe downwards be
aware that God also has given birth to lights in you, and
that they are created in an inner harmony of relationship.
Repeat the words meditatively for 15 minutes.

After the 15 minutes of meditation, begin to express
silently the prayers of your heart. Allow your own heart's
desires to link you with the desire for harmony and
wholeness that is within men and women everywhere. Pray
for them as well. After about five minutes of silent prayer
close with the Lord's prayer or other words.

If you are meditating with others, share together some
of what you have experienced in the silence. This is a time
for listening and for reflecting on what you have heard
within yourself and in one another.

THE FIFTH DAY: THE CREATURELINESS OF GOD

5

The Fifth Day:
The Creatureliness of God

*And God said, 'Let the waters bring forth swarms
of living creatures'.* (Genesis 1:20)

Out of the waters of God's life come the creatures of
earth and sea and sky. They are 'endowed with the five
senses', says Eriugena.[1] With the birth of the creatures
there is the emergence of seeing, hearing, smelling, tasting
and touching. The light of the sun and the whiteness
of the moon can now be seen. The wind blowing through
the leaves of the trees and the crashing of ocean waves
can be heard. The early morning fragrance of the earth
can be smelled. Its fruit can be tasted, and its textures
touched.

This, of course, is not just about the birth of the creatures
but about the gift of our creatureliness and thus the creatureliness of the image in which we have been made. Eriugena says that every creature 'can be called a theophany'.[2]
It is 'the manifestation of the hidden', he says, or 'the
visibility of the invisible'.[3] This is not to say that what is
shown in a creature is the essence of God, for God is
essentially unknowable. Rather, what is manifested is an
expression of God's essence. Nothing in creation exists in
and by itself. The soul of every creature is derived from
the one Soul. God, therefore, is not simply *in* every creature

but is the *essence* of every creature. At heart, creation – including our creatureliness – is a showing forth of the mystery of God.

In a meditation on the theme of the fifth day of creation, one man saw the flow of the river of life. To begin with there were small water creatures and all sorts of fish in the river, but as it flowed past him they became a variety of other creatures until finally there were deer and horses leaping out of the waters. Eriugena says that all created things are like streams issuing from one source. From the beginning of time they have pursued 'their different courses through subterranean channels until they break out above ground in the different forms of the individual objects of nature'.[4] These images speak of the evolution of all things from the invisible waters of God's life.

George MacDonald, in his novel *Lilith*, describes a vision of God that flashes forth from a cloud burst:

> All kinds of creatures – horses and elephants, lions and dogs – oh, such beasts! And such birds! – great birds whose wings gleamed singly every colour gathered in sunset or rainbow! little birds whose feathers sparkled as with all the precious stones of the hoarding earth! – silvery cranes; red flamingoes; opal pigeons; peacocks gorgeous in gold and green and blue; jewelly humming birds! – great-winged butterflies; lithe-volumed creeping things – all in one heavenly flash![5]

What is glimpsed fleetingly is a kaleidoscopic vision of the creaturely realm as a theophany of God.

The Irish monk Columbanus said, 'If you wish to know the Creator, come to know his creatures.' It is interesting to note that Columbanus's sixth-century mission to the Continent included the founding of the monastery of Bobbio in Italy, where St Francis later was trained. One of the common characteristics between Franciscan spirituality and the Celtic tradition is the emphasis placed on a relationship with the creatures. There are many well-known stories of the Celtic saints befriending animals, but what is this tradition asserting about God, and about the divine image in the human, when it contends that the birth of every creature is a theophany?

In part it is pointing to the senses of God, or to God's way of knowing, and to the inner senses of the image in which we have been made. 'To see with the eyes of the heart' is a phrase often used in the Celtic tradition.[6] It speaks of perceiving at dimensions of reality deeper than the outward. The inclusion of creatures in the garden of God in Genesis is pointing not simply to the outward dimension of the creaturely realm. It also is showing something of the way of God's seeing or sensing, and naming the creation of the inner senses in us. Paradise, as Eriugena explains, is not something that we are separated from in time and space. Rather, it represents the place of the true image of God within us, from which we are separated by degrees of wholeness.

Without the use of the inner senses we are cut off from the heart of life, and therefore from a knowledge of God. This is not to say that our inner sight or our inner hearing are infallible. We know how misguided we can be at times in our sense of truth and of what we should or should not do. This, however, will usually have more to do with our neglect of the inner senses than with their fallibility. It is not enough simply to say that the knowledge of God is to be found in the Bible or the Church. Neither of these, nor the book of creation, can be read without the use of the inner faculties of sense. This would be 'as if you were to tell a blind man that he has light to guide him', as Alexander Scott says, or 'as if you were to affirm in regard to a deaf man that he needs not ears because there is a voice speaking to him'.[7]

Our knowledge of God is not an external deposit of truth, watched over in unaltered form from age to age by the authority of the Church. Rather, it is an experience of God that comes to us in the use of our inner senses, whether that be through the scriptures and sacraments or through creation and one another. It is not a doctrinal or propositional knowledge, says Scott, but belongs 'to some deeper part of the human being'.[8] It is like the way an infant comes to know its mother:

> What do its senses reveal? Forms, colours, motions, sounds: these are not a soul, but through these it detects the presence of a soul, answering to its soul . . . Even thus does a knowledge of the Highest Spirit come through the universe.[9]

In the Celtic tradition there is the conviction, as we have noted, that our deepest desire is for the Love that is at the heart of life. It is a desire to see, to hear, to smell, to taste and to touch the One whom we desire. While the essence of God is beyond anything that can be seen or handled, creation is the expression of God. It is the divine embodiment that we may sense and touch in love. Confused desires have led us in all sorts of directions in our lives, to such an extent that sometimes we come to believe that the awakening of desire is a dangerous thing. But until the deepest of our desires is addressed we will be like people who are not truly alive. As Kenneth White writes:

> . . . the surface of things
> can give enjoyment or disgust
> but the inwardness of things
> gives life[10]

To speak thus of the inner realm is not to downplay the outer senses, for in the Celtic tradition the physical and the spiritual are inseparably interwoven. Often it will be through our gift of physical sight, for instance, that a grace of inner sight opens within us. Most of us will have experienced this in gazing across an open sea or in watching sunlight dapple through the branches of a tree. At an inner level we find ourselves at such moments sensing something of the boundlessness of life or of its interpenetration by a mystery beyond our comprehension.

Our Western religious inheritance often has led us to mistrust our creatureliness rather than to recognize its essential goodness. Although not many of us will have been taught explicitly that our physical senses are by nature servants of sin, most of us in one way or another will have been discouraged from confidently naming our creatureliness as of God. So aware have we been made of the unruliness of the senses that, when our creatureliness is led astray, we have been given the impression that the problem is our creatureliness rather than its capacity to be unruly.

In a meditation on the gift of our senses, one man saw within himself a net of fish spilling out on to the deck of a ship. They leapt lithely and their sheen of colours glistened in the light. As he watched them he became aware of how uncomfortable he had been made to feel about his own creatureliness, caught in a net of doubt and inhibition. He realized how difficult it was to live with his strength of natural desire when he had been taught to see it essentially as wayward. Many of the features of his creatureliness had become repugnant to him. They were smelly rather than fresh and gleaming like the live fish that he saw in his meditation. Along similar lines, a woman in her meditation saw animals that were held in captivity and prevented from being themselves. She saw the lifeless countenance of a caged lion.

The Celtic tradition does not pretend that the energies of our senses cannot become disordered or even destructive, but always it affirms the essential goodness of the gift of our creatureliness. Eriugena makes the point that on the day of judgement we will not be judged on the basis of what God has created in us – namely, our creatureliness – but on the basis of what God has not created in us, the false use of our senses. 'To lay the blame upon nature', he says, 'is to lay it upon the Creator of nature Himself: if nature is the cause of sin, then God, who is the Cause of nature, must also be the cause of nature's sin.'[11]

Not only are our senses regarded as essentially good, they are viewed as given that we may see and taste and touch the manifestation of God in the body of creation and in our own bodies. The desire for God should not lead to a denial of our creatureliness and a subsequent looking away from life. Rather, it should lead us to the renewing of our senses that we may be aware of God within life and at the very heart of who we are. Pelagius speaks of the grace of Christ washing us with water so that we may be 'more beautiful day by day'.[12] Redemption, in this way of seeing, is about returning to our senses. It is about becoming truly alive. The gift of grace is not opposed to the gift of nature. Rather, it restores us to the true gift of our creatureliness

The image that came to one woman in meditation was of lying naked in a cave beside a fire. A swan with a broken wing lay against her. She was aware of her neck growing and of feathers forming on her body. She had become a swan, a creature of great strength and beauty, and began to fly. These images speak of the woundedness of our creatureliness as well as its natural beauty. They speak also of the strength that is in us waiting to be set free.

There are many stories that associate the great Celtic saints with the creatures of earth and sea and sky. Some of them are more fantastic than others. Coleman, for instance, is said to have befriended three animals. A cock woke him up for early morning prayer, a mouse nibbled at his toes if he did not get up, and a fly acted as a pre-computer cursor to indicate which line of the Psalter he should be singing! In many of the old legends it was animals who would lead the saints to their places of new beginnings and mission. The impression given is that the creatures, fully alive in their senses, were more alert than the saints to the guidance of God and the dangers of the journey.

We have noted already how Celtic art interweaves images from the whole of creation into its illuminations of Gospel manuscripts and its stone-carvings of high crosses. The Book of Kells, perhaps the greatest of the great Celtic Gospel Books, depicts every conceivable type of creature on its decorative 'carpet' pages as well as between the lines of Gospel text itself. Some of the depictions are realistic and even humorous, such as that at the beginning of St Matthew's Gospel in which two cats sit quietly watching two rats gnawing at a church wafer. Elsewhere the images suddenly twist and turn fantastically so that the creaturely, the human and the angelic merge into one, which of course reflects the Celtic awareness of the inter-relatedness of life.

Particularly sacred to the Celts, both in Christian and pre-Christian legend, are birds. Two of the most cherished saints in Celtic spirituality – St John the Evangelist and St Columba of Iona – were identified with the creatures of the air. The Gospel writer's mystical insights often are associated with the vision and sharpness of an eagle's eye, and Columba's name, 'Columcille', means 'the dove of the Church'. It was typical of Celtic Christianity to adapt to the Church's usage symbolism that had sacred associations in its pre-Christian cultural past. One of the most significant examples of this is the use of bird imagery to represent the soul of Christ. In some of the Irish high-cross carvings, the depiction of the Easter morning visitation of women to the tomb shows a bird re-entering the mouth of Christ to bring back life.

In legends of pre-Christian origin, messengers from the other-world often appear in bird disguise. 'Shape-shifting', as it came to be known, is a recurring image in Celtic tales. It conveys a sense of the fluidity of the material realm and of the mysterious inter-relatedness of the seen with the unseen. It is one of the many themes of Celtic legend that George MacDonald adapted to his nineteenth-century story-telling. Mr Raven, for instance, in *Lilith*, is a messenger from the spiritual world who is able to move back and forth between the visible and invisible. The ability of birds to shift rapidly from air to earth, or from sea to air, makes them powerful images of the communion between heaven and earth. Such is the nature of the six-winged creatures around the throne of God in Ezekiel's vision in scripture or the images that covered the ceiling of the inner sanctuary in Solomon's temple, of cherubim spreading their wings in flight.[13]

Part of what is communicated in the Celtic tradition is simply a greater awareness of the creatures. During my time on Iona we lived in a house called Dunsmeorach, which means 'The Hill of the Thrush'. An old Gaelic speaker of Iona told me how the house had come to be so named. When the men of the island were constructing it, a mother thrush built her nest in one of the walls and there laid her eggs. So attentive were the men to the life of the bird that they left off building that particular wall until the young had flown. And so the house that sits on a hillock opposite the Abbey is called Dunsmeorach, 'The Hill of the Thrush'. It is a story that points to the attentiveness to creation that is so typical of the Celtic tradition as a whole.

It would be wrong to give the impression that the creation awareness of Celtic spirituality is only of beautifully innocent creatures. As much as the Celtic tradition in recent years has been represented in such terms, it is not at heart a romantic tradition. Part of its reverencing of the natural world is a respect also for creation's wildness and power. It knows this not only in relation to the animal world out there, as it were, but to the creaturely depths of who we are. The great sea monsters that are celebrated in its poetry and prayers reside not just in the hidden depths of the seas but in the recesses of our own nature. The naming of these as part of the mystery is neither to negate their fierceness nor to attempt to tame their wildness. It is to be aware of their power.

The story of St Columba encountering the sea monster of Loch Ness makes this point. When the saint sees that a boy swimming across the loch is being threatened by the great creature he rebukes it. He does not kill the monster, nor does he try to tame it. Rather, he confronts its power of destructiveness in order to save the boy. The Celtic tradition is not naive to the capacity for destruction that lies hidden in the creaturely. It respects this power by being alert to it, but does not thereby define the creaturely solely in terms of danger. The sea monster, too, is a theophany of God.

The Book of Job says, 'Ask the animals, and they will teach you; the birds of the air, and they will tell you.'[14] To look to the animal world is not to look away from God. In the Celtic tradition the creation mystery is part of the Christ mystery. As St Paul says, 'In him all things in heaven and on earth were created'.[15] They are part of what is fully

expressed in him. As the Word or utterance of God, Christ
shows us the truth of creation that we have become separated from. He shows us the goodness of our creatureliness,
calling us to reclaim it rather than deny it.

George MacDonald, in his short-story 'The Golden Key',
explores the theme of the recovery of our senses. Redemption for him includes a listening to creation and a re-establishing of our relationship with the creatures. The
little girl of the story, in the presence of the wise and
beautiful grandmother figure who is an image of the divine,
begins to hear the creatures in a new way:

> They were no longer sounds only; they were speech, and
> speech that she could understand . . . She understood all
> that they said, though she could not repeat a word of
> it.[16]

Part of the recovery of our relationship with creation
involves a willingness to listen in new ways, and in listening
to be prepared to open ourselves at levels that cannot be
translated easily into human speech and thought.

One of the keys to listening needs to be simply an
appreciative attentiveness to the creatures. Kenneth White
provides many examples of this in his poetry. In 'A Short
Introduction to White Poetics' he writes:

> Consider first the Canada Goose,
> brown body, whitish breast
> black head, long black neck . . .
>
> Then there's the Barnacle Goose . . .
> flight note
> a rapidly repeated *gnuk*:
> *gnuk gnuk gnuk gnuk gnuk gnuk gnuk*
> (like an ecstatic Eskimo) . . .

The Snow Goose
has a pure white plumage
with blacktipped wings . . .
in Europe you might take her for a swan
or maybe a gannet
till she lets you know abruptly
with one harsh *kaank*
she's all goose

so
there they go
through the wind, the rain, the snow

wild spirits
knowing what they know[17]

There are so many things that we need to re-learn from
the creatures that will only come through the delight of
attentively observing them: their ability to be still, for
instance, and in that stillness to have a heightened awareness of what is around them; or the way in which an animal
sometimes will lie motionless when it is wounded. In a
meditation on this theme I saw within me an injured deer
lying in the heather. Her eyes were open and still. In her
suffering she was watching and waiting for a healing that
would come out of the stillness.

There is also the unbroken song of the creatures. St John
the Divine envisages an unending song of praise being sung
by all that swims and flies and has motion. The four living
creatures gathered around the throne of God in the Book
of Revelation, 'each of them with six wings' and 'full of
eyes all around and inside', represent the creatures of earth
and sea and sky. Quivering with a vitality of life and consciousness they sing, 'Holy, holy, holy, the Lord God the
Almighty, who was and is and is to come.'[18] As a woman

in the *Carmina Gadelica* tradition is recorded as saying, 'Every creature on the earth here below and in the ocean beneath and in the air above was giving glory to the great God of the creatures and the worlds . . . and would *we* be dumb!'[19]

Much of that ceaseless praise, of course, cannot be heard, for it is expressed not in words but in being. It is the delight of a fulmar riding the wind. It is the faithfulness of a blackbird to her young. It is the mysterious awareness of starlings in flight to the swarm's every shift and change of direction. As Kenneth White writes in his 'Epistle to the Birds of this Coast':

> please keep on using the sky
> as you know how
> riding the wind
> with your eyes wide open
> tracing out the shoreline
> (along with something else it's harder to define)
> and throw out a cry or two now and then
> for those of us down here who care
> that'll be a kind of reminder
> (to accompany the signs
> we read silent in the stone):
> way beyond the heart's house
> right into the bone[20]

Exercise

Meditating is a way of being alert to the senses that God has woven into our being, both physically and spiritually.

Begin your time of meditation by finding the right position and the right place, whether that be inside or out of doors. Be intentional about choosing or creating the space that will be most conducive to meditating on both scripture and creation.

Repeat silently the words derived from Job 12, 'Ask the creatures, they will tell you'. At the same time allow images and memories of creatures and of the human senses to be recalled within you.

If you wish to use your breathing to set the rhythm of repetition, try saying the words, 'Ask the creatures, they will tell you', as you breathe upwards. Feel your body expanding. Know that in meditative prayer we are opening ourselves to the One who dwells deep within us. We can listen to Wisdom being spoken from those depths. 'Ask the creatures, they will tell you.' Then as you breathe downwards be aware of the gift of your creatureliness and of the inner senses that God has placed within you. Repeat the words meditatively for 15 minutes as a way of being reawakened within yourself.

After the 15 minutes of meditation, begin to express silently the prayers of your heart. Allow your own heart's desires to link you with the longings of men and women throughout the world to be more fully alive within themselves as well as in their bodies and relationships. Pray for them as well. After about five minutes of silent prayer close with the Lord's prayer or other words.

If you are meditating with others, share together some of what you have experienced in the silence. This is a time for listening and for reflecting on what you have heard within yourself and in one another.

THE
SIXTH DAY:
THE
IMAGE OF GOD

6

The Sixth Day:
The Image of God

God created humankind in his image, in the image of God he created them; male and female he created them. (Genesis 1:27)

On the sixth day humanity is born, in the 'image' and 'likeness' of God, says Genesis.[1] The emergence of man and woman brings creation to a fullness of birth, for humanity contains within itself the mystery of all that has been created. The creatureliness of the fifth day and the masculinity and femininity of the sun and moon have a place in humanity. Similarly, the earth's 'beautiful firmness', the swirling elemental movements of creativity and the light of the first day all find expression in the creation of humanity.

We are created, writes George MacDonald, 'not out of nothing ... but out of God's own endless glory'.[2] This is one of the points at which the Celtic tradition significantly diverges from the Western tradition at large. We are created out of the essence of God, not out of nothing. So essential is the Being of God to our being that if God's life were somehow extracted from our life we would cease to exist. Alexander Scott compared this interweaving of the divine in the human to the thread that was woven through royal garments in the nineteenth century. It could not be removed without the cloth being entirely destroyed. So it is in the being of humanity. There is woven through us a fibre of 'royal nature', said Scott, the removal of which would be our total disintegration.[3]

To say that we are made in the image of the divine is to say that what is deepest in us is of God. At the heart of who we are is the love of God, the wisdom of God, the creativity, imagination and wildness of God. 'What is most human', says Scott, is 'the most divine: what is most divine, the most human'.[4] God is not present '*beside* the human merely, but *in* the human'.[5] 'The Infinite', he says, is 'consubstantiated with the human.'[6] The extent to which we fail to reflect the image of God in our lives is the extent to which we have become less than truly human.

To believe that we are born in God's likeness is to believe that what is deepest in us is mystery. Just as the essence of God is 'invisible and incomprehensible and passes all understanding', says Eriugena, so it is with humanity, created in God's image.[7] What *cannot* be known about us is greater by far than what *can* be known. The deeper we delve into the mystery of our being the more we become aware of its limitless depths. This is not to preclude a scientific study and investigation of the human. Rather, it is to say that the heart of who we are always surpasses knowledge. We can be 'contained within no definition', says Eriugena.[8] This perspective in the Celtic tradition leads to a reverencing of human nature. No one is to be regarded merely as an object, for at heart each woman and man is a holy mystery.

One of the ways in which the Celtic tradition points to the mystery that is deep within us is to speak of 'the trinity of our nature'. Even in the pre-Christian Celtic world there had been a love of triads. The sacred number three was baptized by the Celtic mission into the heart of its teachings concerning the mysteries of God and humanity. There is the legend of St Patrick using the three-leaf clover to suggest the threefold mystery of the unity of God.

Eriugena further develops the Celtic love of unity in trinity when he describes humanity as being formed in 'the image and likeness of the creative Trinity'.[9] The whole of our being reflects the image of the Father, the image of the Son and the image of the Holy Spirit. In other words, there is no part of our being that is not rooted in the creating, redeeming and inspiring mystery of God. There are particular dimensions of who we are, however, that specifically reflect one face of the trinity more than another. The *essence* of our being reflects the first person of the Trinity, the universal Father or Mother in whom all things have their origin. The *expression* of our being reflects the Child of God who is the utterance of Love. And the *operation* of our being and our capacity for creativity and new beginnings reflects the Spirit who in the beginning stirred forth life from the darkness of the waters. To speak of the trinity of our nature is not to suggest that we can define our being in doctrines or formulas. Rather, it is to say that the mystery of the Trinity is the ground of our own mystery, both individually and collectively.

The Genesis account moves swiftly from the creation of Adam and Eve towards what has come to be known as 'the Fall'. Humanity sins and thereby loses its innocence and is forced to leave the garden of Eden. Let us be very clear, however, that by 'loss of innocence' the Celtic tradition does not mean an erasing or destroying of the holy image. The divine likeness within us may be hidden or forgotten. It may be held in terrible bondage by wrongdoing but the image of God remains at the heart of who we are, even though we may live at what seems an infinite distance from it. We have distorted the image but not erased it. 'The integrity of human nature', says Eriugena, 'in no man is destroyed although in all men save Christ is defiled.'[10] The failures of our lives and the falseness of what we have become do not have the power to undo what God has woven into the very fabric of our nature.

Redemption in this model of spirituality is about recovering the treasure that is buried deep in the field of our lives. Even when it lies largely obscured, the image of God, which by its very nature is immortal and indestructible, can be glimpsed within us and among us. Pelagius argued that this alone accounts for the goodness and wisdom that we have known and experienced in the lives of those who make no claim to be recipients of Christ's grace. Pelagius also points to the knowledge of good and evil that is planted within every human being. Why is it, he asks, that people blush or feel guilty when they have committed a wrongdoing?

> Why else unless it is because nature itself is its own witness and discloses its own good by the very fact of its disapproval of evil? ... Hence it comes about that frequently, though a murderer's identity remains concealed, torments of conscience make furious attacks on the author of the crime, and the secret punishment of the mind takes vengeance on the guilty man in hiding.[11]

There is, says Pelagius, a type of natural sanctity within us that knows when we have done what is good and when we have done what is wrong. He compares this to St Paul's reference in Romans to those outside Judaism who instinctively do what the law commands. 'They show that what the law requires is written on their hearts,' says Paul.[12] This instinctive knowledge is part of the image of God in us. It has not been erased by our disobedience, but rather obscured or dulled.

Most of us will have experienced glimpsing something

of the glory of God's image in unexpected people and places. In meditating on this theme one man remembered finding a person whom he knew lying drunk in a gutter. As well as the surprise of discovering an old acquaintance in an alcoholic condition, he was startled by the look of trust that came from the man's eyes. Deeper than the degrading exterior of what this man had become was the integrity that lay hidden within him. Similarly, another person in meditation recalled seeing an old woman in the late stages of dementia. Fleetingly he saw the dignity that was in this woman, shrouded as it was by a terrible confusion in her countenance. So it is at times within ourselves. In the midst of our own inner confusions we sometimes catch glimpses of our true nature. These glimpses beckon us to return to ourselves.

The garden of God in which we have been created has not been destroyed. Nor has it been abandoned. We may live in a state of exile from it, but God forever dwells in that place and seeks our company. The Book of Genesis describes God as 'walking in the garden at the time of the evening breeze' and calling out 'Where are you?'[13] The garden, says Eriugena, is our 'human nature that was made in the image of God'.[14] God, he says, still walks in the garden of our souls searching for us:

This is the voice of the Creator rebuking human nature. It is as if He said: Where are you now after your transgression? For I do not find you there where I know that I created you, nor in that dignity in which I made you in My image and likeness, but I rebuke you as a deserter from blessedness, a fugitive from the true light, hiding yourself in the secret places of your conscience, and I enquire into the cause of your disobedience ... For if you had not eaten [the forbidden fruit] perhaps you would not fear the voice of your Creator as He walks within you, nor flee from His face, nor have become aware of the nakedness which you lost when you sinned.[15]

We have covered ourselves with the false complexity of sin rather than living out of the true simplicity of what we are at heart. Eriugena defines falseness as seeking to be what we are not, or appearing other than we truly are.[16] The voice in the garden of our soul asks, 'Where are you? Why have you lost confidence in the naked beauty of the image in which you have been made?'

Although the Celtic tradition emphasizes that the image of God in us is everlasting and therefore cannot be erased, it is not thereby naive to the deeply destructive implications of sin. The foundations of our being may not have been destroyed by sin but they have been shaken at the deepest level. 'Most mighty and most wretched was that fall', says Eriugena, by which our human nature descended into 'a profound ignorance of herself and her Creator'.[17] So extreme is the departure from our true selves that we forget more and more the image in which we have been made. Eriugena calls this the 'soul's forgetfulness'.[18]

Forgetful of who we are, we live out of ignorance instead of wisdom, fear instead of love, and fantasy instead of reality. The more we forget that the image of God is the deepest reality within us, the less we delve into those inner depths for the gifts of God. The less we make use of the spiritual resources implanted at the heart of our being the more we come to believe that they are not there. And the less we believe that such riches are within us the more we treat ourselves and one another with a lack of respect. As Pelagius advises Demetrias, a person must first recognize within herself the presence of God's gifts, 'which she will be able to employ to the full only when she has learned that she possesses them'.[19] To know with an inner confidence the gift of God's image within us is very different, of course, from having an inflated sense of self. The latter is as false in the one direction as a sense of self-worthlessness is in the other. The beauty and dignity of our true self is gift.

George MacDonald, in his novel *Lilith*, describes the dull and ugly giants of the land in which no waters flow as 'staring through a fog'.[20] Not only do they not see clearly enough to be able to detect in their midst the presence of 'the little ones', who still live in a state of innocence and joy, but also they do not remember once having been little ones themselves. Similarly, *Lilith*, who in the Jewish Kabbalah tradition is the first wife of Adam, is described by MacDonald as so distant from her true self that she confuses the evil will of the Shadow for her own will. 'I will be myself and not another,' she says in response to a call for repentance. 'Alas,' says the messenger of love, 'you are another now, not yourself! Will you not be your real self?'[21]

Our tendency, as Alexander Scott says, is to 'doubt or deny' the attributes of the image of God that are part of the foundation of our being.[22] The gospel is given to restore our memory of what lies deepest within us. In a meditation on this theme, reflecting on words from the Book of Psalms,

> Yet you have made them a little lower than God,
> and crowned them with glory and honour.[23]

one man saw himself again and again throwing down the crown of glory. He was refusing to accept the gift of God's image within himself. Another man, in meditating on these words, remembered the magnificent staircase of a public art gallery. He saw people going up and down the stairs clinging insecurely to the side as if they were not worthy of the grandeur of the staircase. We readily disbelieve that the dignity of God's image is planted within us, preferring instead to live out of our sense of failure and unworthiness. Of course, there is much in us that is unworthy. We have failed even those whom we most cherish in life. But do we know that deeper still is the loveliness of who we are, made in the image of God? The Scriptures refer to God as 'the king of beauty'.[24] The Celtic tradition wants to say that at heart we are princes or princesses of beauty.

Pelagius, in his letter to Demetrias, advises her that the lower opinion we have of ourselves the less we will be capable of a true self-reverencing. To another woman he writes, 'have regard for your origin, consider your lineage, respect the honour of your noble stock. Acknowledge you are not only the daughter of a man but the daughter of God as well, graced with the nobility of divine birth.'[25] To know these depths within ourselves is an important part of recognizing them also in others and of acting accordingly. 'To God nothing is so offensive,' writes Pelagius, 'nothing so detestable as to hate anyone and to want to injure anyone; nothing is so commendable in his sight as to love everyone.'[26] An essential aspect of reverencing the image of God in others is to refrain from disparaging them or even from believing another's words of disparagement. 'This practice of disparagement', says Pelagius, 'is a very grave fault, because it makes another appear worthless, and you are to avoid defamation with the ears no less than the tongue.'[27]

Not only does the Celtic tradition see sin as the soul's forgetfulness of itself, but as an infection deep within us. Eriugena calls it a 'leprosy of the soul'.[28] It is an infection that distorts the beauty of the image of God. As leprosy disfigures the skin and grotesquely alters the human countenance, so sin distorts the face of the soul. It can produce a madness or monstrous appearance in us that bears only the slightest resemblance to our true self. It is 'like some strange face', says Eriugena, that 'takes its own form'.[29]

So blurred has our impression of the human soul become that when we are false or selfish it often is said of us that we are merely acting according to human nature. The Celtic tradition wants to say emphatically that such failure is not human nature but a distortion of it. 'It is not nature herself who has sinned', says Eriugena, but an unruly use of the will moving 'irrationally against nature':[30]

> For in itself evil is a deformity and an abhorrent ugliness which, if the erring sense beheld undisguised, it would not only refuse to follow or take delight in, but would flee from and abhor. But the unwitting sense errs, and in erring is deceived, because it takes the evil for something which is good and fair to look upon and pleasant to taste.[31]

Our failings and inhumanities to one another are not manifestations of what human nature produces. Rather, they represent a perversion of our nature, using 'the good in the wrong way', as Eriugena says.[32]

How is it, then, that we are restored to our true selves? Eriugena speaks of 'the medicine of Divine Grace' which will restore our soul's memory and heal our deep infection:

> As the skin of the human body is smitten by the ugly contagion of leprosy, so human nature is infected and ... becomes unlike its Creator. But when by the medicine of the Divine Grace it shall be cured of that leprosy, then shall it be restored to its former beauty; what is more, in itself the nature which was created in the Image of God never did lose the bloom of its beauty nor the

integrity of its essence, nor could it do so: for the divine form ... itself ever remains immutable.[33]

Commenting on the Gospel story of the ten lepers who are healed by Jesus, Eriugena says that it is not that they ever lost their true countenance. Rather, it was that their faces had been 'covered up by the tumours and filthiness of the leprosy'. From this 'we are to understand', he says, 'that our nature is neither lost nor changed, but tarnished'.[34] The face once 'obscured by the disease shines forth in health again'.[35]

In meditating on the theme of what it means to be restored to the image of God within us, one woman saw herself as bound with a blackness that clung to her like ashes. The ashes needed to be brushed away. Another imagined that she was covered with a strange papery garment. Although it was thin it entirely obscured her naturalness. A more modern image was of a computer's floppy disc that had become fragmented. Its contents were totally disordered. Restoration meant a re-ordering of the disc from within the computer's memory. Such images speak of salvation as a re-establishing in us of what is deepest. In the Celtic tradition God's gift of grace is viewed as restoring us to our natural well-being. The gift of nature and the gift of grace are both of God.

But where specifically does the Celtic tradition look for the medicine of grace? Above all else it is to the person of Christ. He presents us with what is truly human.

Alexander Scott, who speaks of the 'naturalness of Christ', uses the metaphor of a botanist examining a plant and finding flaws and dead spots on its leaves. Even if the botanist has not known such a plant before, he will conclude that these are not natural to the plant but have come from some other source. So it is, says Scott, when we look at the men and women of the world:

We see in them humanity, but we see something that has stained, or restricted, or distorted humanity; and if we would conceive of man as he came from the hand of God, we conceive of something different from this; we leave out, in our idea, those breaks and excrescences. One comes who calls himself 'The Son of Man'; he calls us to observe his human life, and see that life without these flaws and distortions . . . He excels us, not in that He is less truly Man than we, but that He is Man in very truth.[36]

Christ restores our memory of what is truly natural. As Eriugena says, he 'is our epiphany'.[37] He shows us our true self. In order to break free from the falseness with which we have clothed ourselves, or the failings which we have defined ourselves in terms of, we need to see what the true face of our soul is. And so in Christ we are shown that we are born of God, bearers of the eternal wisdom and beauty that were conceived with us in our mother's womb.

Christ leads us towards the heart of humanity, not into a type of separation from it. In the nineteenth century, when Western Christianity was not only fragmenting into more and more denominations but generally regarding itself as over and against the rest of humanity, the Celtic tradition called for a new sense of the unity that is at the heart of all people. Instead of being called *Roman* Catholics or *Anglo*-Catholics, by which we define ourselves in terms of a separateness from the rest of humanity, let us be called '*Human* Catholics', said Alexander Scott, for Christ reveals the truth of what is at the heart of humanity.[38] We have been given the gospel not to tell us that there are flaws and spots in our humanity, for we more or less know that about ourselves. Rather, we have been given the gospel to tell us what we do not know about ourselves, or what our souls have forgotten. Deeper than the failings of our lives is the blessing of our nature. It is to that blessedness that we are called to be reconnected.

Pelagius speaks about being 'instructed by the grace of Christ'.[39] Christ reveals that the love and eternal wisdom of God are deep within our human nature, even when they have not been consciously detected or visibly manifested in our lives. The Celtic tradition emphasizes the revelatory nature of Christ's work. He liberates us by showing us God's Self and our true self. This is significantly different from the models of substitutionary atonement that have prevailed in the Western tradition's understanding of Christ. It is important to note that, while the Celtic tradition accentuates the revelatory rather than the substitutionary nature of Christ's redemptive work, there is no less emphasis on the cost of sacrifice. The ultimate revelation of God's love is shown in the self-giving of Christ on the cross. His death is not thereby viewed as any less costly or redemptive.

Part of receiving Christ's grace of revelation is an experience of judgement, for in the light of the truth we see the falseness of what we have become. Eriugena understands judgement not in an external sense but as our conscience being illumined by the light of God. Even in relation to the final judgement, Eriugena says:

> We should not interpret this as meaning that He [God] moves through space [to judge us] . . . but that each man, good and evil, shall behold His coming in himself, in his own conscience, when they shall be set free, and God shall reveal the hidden places of the darkness and each man shall be the judge of his own deeds and thoughts.[40]

The inner experience of truth has the power to set us free, for it reveals not only the falseness that is within us but

[handwritten margin notes: NB; anselm?; marcus Borg]

[handwritten note at bottom: See Troy Watson "New Wisdom"; Grim..... "Instead of atonement"]

the beauty and goodness that are deeper still. It moves us, says Pelagius, 'to be restored by repentance'.[41] In repenting we turn around, not to become someone other than ourselves but to become truly ourselves.

George MacDonald, in his novel *Lilith*, paints a powerful picture of repentance as a journey of return to ourselves. The princess Lilith is so distant from her true nature that she has become enslaved by evil. She has a wound in her side, however, that will not heal until she repents. The wound is her place of vulnerability to truth. Like the 'two-edged sword' of Hebrews that pierces our hearts not to punish us but to cut away what is false,[42] Lilith's wound is penetrated by a 'white-hot' snake that MacDonald calls 'the live heart of essential fire'.[43] It pierces through 'the joints and marrow to the thoughts and intents of the heart'. When it enters the secret chamber of her heart the princess writhes in pain for she sees what she has become. The sword that in the end is used to sever what is false in her from what is true is a sword of 'healing', says MacDonald.[44]

Eriugena says that 'everything which is true is totally indestructible'.[45] Nothing, therefore, that has been created by God will be condemned but only that which has not been created by God, namely our sin and falseness:

And so the great feast [at the end of time] will be ordered and celebrated, from which the substance of no man shall be rejected, for the substance was made by God; and to which the wickedness of no man shall be admitted, for the wickedness was not made by God. For our nature shall be purified, the vice shall be winnowed away, the grain, which is our substance, shall be stored, the stubble, which is sin, shall burn in the flame of the Divine Judgment, the places hid in darkness shall be illuminated, and God shall be seen as all in all.[46]

Even the substance of the devil, says Eriugena, will not be destroyed, for he was created as an angel of light. Like humanity he is evil only in so far as he is false to his true nature.

The repentance that accompanies the gift of grace restores us to the well-being of our human nature. That includes a recollection of the desires that have been planted within us, the deepest of which is the desire for God. We may not be conscious of it, and our search for satisfaction may lead us into all sorts of confused and destructive behaviour. The desire for God, however, has not been erased. Even in the midst of our most terrible 'sins and perversities', says Eriugena, we are longing for God while at the same time not knowing what it is we long for.[47] The desire is for Love, the Love that is at the beginning and heart of all life. As George MacDonald says, 'love, not hate, is deepest in what Love loved into being'.[48] The redemptive hope in the Celtic tradition is of being reawakened to that desire.

Exercise

Meditating is a way of growing in an awareness of the image of God within us.

Begin your time of meditation by finding the right position and the right place, whether that be on your own or in the company of others. Be intentional about choosing or creating the space that will be most conducive to meditating on scripture and on the mystery of humanity.

Repeat silently the words derived from Psalm 8, 'I have crowned you with dignity.' At the same time allow images and memories of the dignity that you have known in others and in yourself to be recalled within you.

If you wish to use your breathing to set the rhythm of repetition, try saying the words, 'I have crowned you with dignity,' as you breathe upwards. Feel your body and the crown of your head expanding. Know that in meditative prayer we are listening to the One who speaks from the depth of our being. Listen to these words of assurance and open yourself to them. 'I have crowned you with dignity.' Then as you breathe downwards be still and allow yourself to be renewed in the dignity of the image in which you are made. Repeat the words meditatively for 15 minutes.

After the 15 minutes of meditation, begin to express silently the prayers of your heart. Allow your own heart's desires to link you with men and women everywhere, and the longing for respect and dignity that is in all people. Pray for them as well. After about five minutes of silent prayer close with the Lord's prayer or other words.

If you are meditating with others, share together some of what you have experienced in the silence. This is a time for listening and for reflecting on what you have heard within yourself and in one another.

THE
SEVENTH DAY:
THE STILLNESS
OF GOD

7

The Seventh Day:
The Stillness of God

God blessed the seventh day and hallowed it, because on it God rested from all the work that he had done in creation. (Genesis 2:3)

The story of the seventh day points to the restfulness of God. It is not opposed to the wild creative energies of the second day, but is the revealing of another dimension of God's creativity. The seven days of Genesis, as we have noted, are not a chronological account of the emergence of the universe in the past but a meditation on the ever-present mystery of creation. The life of creation is a theophany of God. It is a visible expression of the One who is essentially invisible, an intelligible sign of the One who is beyond knowledge. Just as the first day points to the light that is always at the heart of life, so the seventh reflects the stillness that is part of God's ongoing creativity.

This is a pattern that we find woven through the whole of creation. Night is followed by day, sleeping by waking. Similarly in the rhythm of the seasons, the winter earth and its stillness is followed by the spring's energy and blossom. The time of infolding is related to the period of unfolding. The fallowness of the ground is part of the earth's cycle of fruitfulness and abundance. The one does not occur without the other. Creation's outward profusion of life is rooted in its inner capacity for rest and renewal. As Alexander Scott says, the oak that is expanding with growth and forming a new layer of wood is at the same time condensing and 'strengthening its rings toward the heart'.[1] So is creativity related to stillness.

Eriugena speaks of 'the seminal force' that is within the earth.[2] It is part of plant life and animal life as well as human life. The hidden energy of a seed is prepared over periods of relative stillness, whereas its expression is a bursting forth over shorter periods of time. These are followed by intervals of regenerative resting so that in time more seed can be produced. Without the rhythm of restfulness and production the earth's cycles of life would break down.

In the Genesis account of creation a refrain occurs after each day. 'There was evening and there was morning', it says. The day is seen as coming out of the night. The energy and creativity of the daytime emerge from the dark stillness and restfulness of the night. As George MacDonald says, 'the day begins with sleep'.[3] If we are to be creative in the day we must first give ourselves up to the silence of the night.

As the pattern of restfulness and creativity is seen to be part of the nature of God, so is this combination woven through the fabric of human nature, made in the image of God. The extent to which we are divorced from the complementary rhythms of restfulness and creativity is the extent to which we are cut off from patterns of well-being within ourselves and in our relationships. If we fail to establish regular practices of stillness and rest our creativity will be either exhausted or shallow. Our countenance, instead of reflecting a vitality of fresh creative energy that is sustained by the restorative depths of stillness, will be listless or frenetic. This is as true collectively as it is individually, and applies as much to human creativity as it does to the earth's fruitfulness. Creativity without rest, and productivity without renewal, leads to an exhaustion of inner resources.

We all have experienced the sense of well-being that accompanies an integration of restfulness and creative energy. We know the rejuvenation, as well as healing power, that can come out of a good night's sleep. Similarly we have memories, even if they are as far back as child-hood, of the wholesomeness of dropping into bed after a day of straightforward physical exertion. Deep in the gift of creation there is a pattern of relationship between the surging and the renewing of life's energies. It is like the goodness of passionate love-making followed by the heavy restfulness of the body and soul.

Some of the most beautiful prayers in the Celtic tradition are night benedictions. Their intimate inclusion of the Trinity indicates a reverencing of sleep. Rest is viewed almost in sacramental terms:

> I lie down this night with God,
> And God will lie down with me;
> I lie down this night with Christ,
> And Christ will lie down with me;
> I lie down this night with Spirit,
> And the Spirit will lie down with me;
> God and Christ and the Spirit
> Be lying down with me.[4]

The prayers are unusual, not only in their portrayal of God as One who rests, but in their sense of personal intimacy with the Trinity. They do not thereby lose an awareness of the otherness of God. This is not a sentimental piety, nor does the tradition excessively anthropomorphize the Unknowable. God is present to us and to the whole of creation in our times of stillness. Dimensions within us are renewed. Restoring energies are given to us in the night.

In sleep we participate in the way of God, for the restfulness of sleep is regenerative. We need to die to the outwardness of the day in order to be renewed within. To enter stillness, whether in sleep or in wakefulness, is to forget at one level in order to remember at another. It is the way a child, for instance, will lie in the grass gazing up into the skies, forgetting everything else. Only by letting go of other thoughts are we able to be present fully to the wonder of the moment. Children, too, in their capacity to daydream, are reminders to us of the serenity that we have experienced in half-sleeping moments of restfulness. The *Carmina Gadelica* tradition speaks of 'the angeling of my rest'.[5] This points to the time of rest as holy, and therefore as surrounded and protected by the messengers of God, as well as to the grace of renewal and creativity that can emerge out of stillness. The gift of being renewed in such a way comes not only through resting but through the dreams and imaginations of sleep and stillness. To be alert to these is to be open to creative depths within ourselves, stirring us to fresh perspectives and new awareness.

There is a lovely story in the Celtic tradition of Mary and the Christ-child journeying through the Hebrides. On one of the island roads they meet a milk-maid, whom Mary asks to hold the child so that she may rest a while. The milk-maid declines, claiming that she has ten cows to attend to. Further along the road they meet a second milk-maid, who agrees to hold the child for a time. She sings a lullaby to him and suckles him on her breast. Although she has twice as many cows as the first milk-maid, she finishes her day's work in half the time and with four times as much milk! It is a story that points to the relationship between rest and productivity. The rewards of finding a balance between stillness and busyness may not always be so obvious in our lives! Nevertheless we have known the creative energy that comes out of sleep and stillness and the dissipation of energy that results from not resting.

We also know that it is at times of stillness within ourselves that we can be alert to the creative depths that are within us. This is when the imagination with its creative and unexpected ideas flows best. True creativity is not something that we can force out, but only let out. This is not to deny that often it is the energy and stimulation of a demanding moment that will draw forth creativity from us. If we are tired or tense in that moment, however, it is unlikely that our response will be imaginative. Some of our most creative problem solving, like many of the greatest scientific discoveries and artistic conceptions, have occurred not in the midst of directly grappling with the issue at hand but in disengaging. Often it is when we step back or let go that our creativity awakens most fully.

The Irish phrase 'pillow talk' refers to the type of disengaged sharing that can happen at night between a man and a woman as they talk about the concerns of their family or relationship. Lying together in bed, away from the pressure and intensity of the day's busyness, they are more open to the intimations of creativity within them. New beginnings are born out of the letting go that rest and love make room for.

Nature has provided us with patterns of stillness and creativity, of night followed by day and fallowness by fruitfulness. As we have noted all along in the Celtic tradition, grace is viewed not as opposed to nature but as a restoration of what is truly natural. Whether within ourselves, or in our relationships with one another and creation, if we have forgotten the integration of rest and creativity we will likely be undermining our own well-being. A lack of rest is destructive of nature's goodness. Like evil it destroys rather than creates. It saps energy instead of building up life forces within us. Grace is given to restore our memory, to remind us of the place that rest has in the sustaining and liberating of our God-given beauty and vitality.

As important as the patterns of outer restfulness are, they point to the even greater significance of inner stillness. We know that when we are unwell within ourselves a night's sleep, no matter how long, is not able to restore us. A deeper rest is required if we are to be renewed at inner depths. This is what Alexander Scott calls being restored at 'the root' rather than merely at 'the branches'.[6] It is being reconnected to the stillness that is at the heart of life.

Meditation in part is about being reconnected to the stillness of God. Early in the Celtic tradition Pelagius speaks of the daily practice of meditation:

There should be a fixed and appointed number of hours when you are more completely free for God and are bound as if by statute to the most intense mental concentration . . . During these hours each day pray in a more private part of the house with the door of your bedchamber shut (Mt. 6:6). Even when you are in the city subject yourself to this discipline of solitude, remove yourself for a while from the company of men and join yourself more closely to God; then, when you return to the sight of your own family, show them the fruits of your reading and prayer.[7]

Pelagius refers to this discipline as an 'exercising' of our souls, for it is intended not to draw us away from life but to strengthen us for a deeper engagement in life. Meditative prayer renews us within so that outwardly we may take up our responsibilities of relationship and commitment:

Let your home be the object of your concern in such a
way that you can still allot a period of respite to your
soul. Choose a convenient place, a little removed from
the noise of the household, to which you can betake
yourself as if to a harbour out of a great storm of cares
and there, in the peace of inner seclusion, calm the turbulent waves of thoughts outside. There let your study
of divine readings be so constant, your alternations in
prayers so frequent ... that you have no trouble in
making up for all the employments of your remaining
time by this spell of freedom from them. Nor do we say
this with the purpose of detaching you from your family;
rather our intention is that in that place you may learn
and meditate as to what kind of person you ought to
show yourself to your own kin.[8]

The practice of Celtic spirituality, however, is not primarily
about set apart times of meditation and prayer. It is distin-
guished above all else by its emphasis on an awareness of
God in the midst of activity. Some of the most well-known
prayers of the Hebrides were recited in the context of work
and daily routine. Prayers were uttered, for instance, at
waking to the light of the day and at rising in the morning:

Thanks to Thee, O God, that I have risen today,
To the rising of this life itself;
May it be to Thine own glory, O God of every gift,
And to the glory of my soul likewise.

O great God, aid Thou my soul
With the aiding of Thine own mercy;
Even as I clothe my body with wool,
Cover Thou my soul with the shadow of Thy wing.

Help me to avoid every sin,
And the source of every sin to forsake;

And as the mist scatters on the crest of the hills,
May each ill haze clear from my soul, O God.[9]

Similarly, prayer was said or chanted at the preparation of the morning fire:

I will kindle my fire this morning
In the presence of the holy angels of heaven . . .

And as the flame caught fire the prayer would continue:

God, kindle Thou in my heart within
A flame of love to my neighbour,
To my foe, to my friend, to my kindred all . . .
O Son of the loveliest Mary,
From the lowliest thing that liveth,
To the Name that is highest of all.[10]

The whole of the day, including everything that will be seen and heard and handled, is committed to God:

Bless to me, O God,
Each thing mine eye sees;
Bless to me, O God,
Each sound mine ear hears;
Bless to me, O God,
Each odour that goes to my nostrils;
Bless to me, O God,
Each taste that goes to my lips;
Each note that goes to my song,
Each ray that guides my way,
Each thing that I pursue,
Each lure that tempts my will,
The zeal that seeks my living soul,
The Three that seek my heart,
The zeal that seeks my living soul,
The Three that seek my heart.[11]

The Celtic tradition, unlike the Calvinism that suppressed it in many parts of the Celtic world, is not sabbatarian in its perspective. The emphasis is not on set apart times of rest, or so-called 'holy' days and 'holy' places that are distinct from every day and every place. Rather, it encourages a type of restful awareness in everything that we do. It is about holding a stillness of perspective in the midst of busyness. It is about being alert to the light of the sun in the midst of morning work or to the mystery of the moon at night. It is about tasting the goodness of God in the fruit of the earth and the love of God on the lips of another. It is about knowing, as Kenneth White writes, that in all things we are 'surrounded by eternity'.[12]

It is perhaps above all else in the Celtic tradition's death prayers that there is a sense of the regenerative nature of rest. Once again, grace is viewed as restoring us to our true selves. The stillness of death alone will bring the depth of sleep that can heal our innermost wounds. The *Carmina Gadelica* refers to death's 'healing balsam' or to the 'salve that is needful for my soul':

> Give Thou to me, O God,
> The death of the priceless oil;
> Give Thou to me, O God,
> That the Healer of my soul be near me;
> Give Thou to me, O God,
> The death of joy and of peace.[13]

What is being sought is life through death, or as one of the prayers says, 'death without death'.[14]

George MacDonald, in his novel *Lilith*, explores the themes of death being the sleep that will restore all things. 'No one who will not sleep', he writes, 'can ever wake.'[15] In the great 'House of Death', in which there are endless rows of beds, the time required for sleep depends on how distant we have become from our true selves. It is a place of forgetting what is false in order to remember what is true. Lilith's sleep is long, writes MacDonald, because 'she is busy forgetting'.[16] In the midst of her redemptive rest, given that she may recover her true nature, dreams play a part in leading her towards a repentance of past wrongs. Only then does the princess regain her original beauty. MacDonald describes a place called 'the Evil Wood', populated by those who refuse to rest. 'It is the place', he writes, 'where those who will not sleep, wake up at night to kill their dead and bury them.'[17] It is a haunt of madness that reflects the self-destructiveness of refusing to be still.

The sleep of death is given not to withdraw us from life but to restore us to the very heart of life, or to 'the home of the seasons' as the *Carmina Gadelica* calls it. In the Celtic tradition of the Hebrides such imagery was used in the prayers chanted at the deathbed of loved ones:

> Thou goest home this night to thy home of winter,
> To thy home of autumn, of spring, and of summer;
> Thou goest home this night to thy perpetual home,
> To thine eternal bed, to thine eternal slumber.

> Sleep thou, sleep, and away with thy sorrow,
> Sleep thou, sleep, and away with thy sorrow,
> Sleep thou, sleep, and away with thy sorrow;
> Sleep, thou beloved, in the Rock of the fold.

> Sleep this night in the breast of thy Mother,
> Sleep, thou beloved, while she herself soothes thee;
> Sleep thou this night on the Virgin's arm,
> Sleep, thou beloved, while she herself kisses thee.

> The great sleep of Jesus, the surpassing sleep of Jesus,
> The sleep of Jesus' wound, the sleep of Jesus' grief,

The young sleep of Jesus, the restoring sleep of Jesus,
The sleep of the kiss of Jesus of peace and of glory.

The sleep of the seven lights be thine, beloved,
The sleep of the seven joys be thine, beloved,
The sleep of the seven slumbers be thine, beloved,
On the arm of the Jesus of blessings, the Christ of
    grace.

The shade of death lies upon thy face, beloved,
But the Jesus of grace has His hand round about thee;
In nearness to the Trinity farewell to thy pains,
Christ stands before thee and peace is in His mind.

Sleep, O sleep in the calm of all calm,
Sleep, O sleep in the guidance of guidance,
Sleep, O sleep in the love of all loves;
Sleep, O beloved, in the Lord of life,
    Sleep, O beloved, in the God of life![18]

While such prayers were known as 'death prayers', they
are more profoundly 'life prayers'. They speak of entering
rest, whether in life or in death, in order to be more alive,
in order to be more awake to the Life that is within all
life.

Exercise

Meditating is a way of being renewed in the stillness of
God within us.

Begin your time of meditation by finding the right position and the right place, whether that be inside or out of
doors. Be intentional about choosing or creating the space

that will be most conducive to meditating on both scripture and creation.

Repeat silently the words from Psalm 46, 'Be still and know that I am God.' At the same time allow images and memories of stillness, from creation as well as from your own life, to be recalled within you.

If you wish to use your breathing to set the rhythm of repetition, try saying the words, 'Be still and know that I am God,' as you breathe upwards. Feel your body expanding. Know that in meditative prayer we are listening to the One who speaks from the stillness at the heart of life. Then as you breathe downwards simply be still and aware of being refreshed in the silence. Repeat the words meditatively for 15 minutes.

After the 15 minutes of meditation, begin to express silently the prayers of your heart. Allow your own heart's desires to connect you with the desire that is in the whole of creation to be renewed through rest. Pray especially for people who are longing for a restorative peace and stillness. After about five minutes of silent prayer close with the Lord's prayer or other words.

If you are meditating with others, share together some of what you have experienced in the silence. This is a time for listening and for reflecting on what you have heard within yourself and in one another.

Notes

Introduction

1 K. White, 'Letter from Harris', in *The Bird Path* (Mainstream, 1989), p. 118.
2 A. J. Scott, *The Social Systems of the Present Day, Compared with Christianity* (Sherwood, 1841), p. 367.
3 Hebrews 4:12.
4 Wisdom 2:23; 8:6.
5 John 1:1–3.
6 John 13:23.
7 See J. P. Newell, *Listening for the Heartbeat of God: A Celtic Spirituality* (SPCK, 1997).
8 See N. Chadwick, *The Celts* (Penguin Books, 1971), p. 51.
9 Ecclesiasticus 1:14.
10 John 1:9.
11 John 8:12.
12 Bede, *Ecclesiastical History of the English People* (Penguin Books, 1990), p. 188.
13 Matthew 16:18.
14 John Scotus Eriugena, *Periphyseon (The Division of Nature)* (Bellarmin, 1987), 749D.
15 Eriugena, *Periphyseon* 681A.
16 John Scotus Eriugena, 'Homily on the Prologue to the Gospel of St John', in *The Voice of the Eagle* (Lindisfarne Press, 1990), p. 37.
17 See A. Carmichael, *Carmina Gadelica* (Constable, 1900); and D. Hyde, *Religious Songs of Connacht* (Gill, 1906).
18 A. J. Scott, *Lectures on the Epistle to the Romans* (Darling, 1838), p. 7.

19 G. MacLeod, *The Whole Earth Shall Cry Glory* (Wild Goose Publications, 1985), p. 13.
20 White, 'Poem to my Coat', in *The Bird Path*, p. 111.
21 Psalm 46:10.
22 White, 'The House of Insight', in *The Bird Path*, p. 141.

1 *The First Day: The Light of God*

1   John 8:12.
2   John 1:9.
3   Eriugena, *Periphyseon* 445D.
4   D. Bohm, *Wholeness and the Implicate Order* (Ark, 1990).
5   Eriugena, *Periphyseon* 681B.
6   R. Ferguson (ed.), *Daily Readings with George MacLeod* (Fount, 1991), p. 68.
7   White, 'The Chaoticist Manifesto', in *The Bird Path*, p. 225.
8   White, 'The House of Insight', in *The Bird Path*, p. 143.
9   Eriugena, *Periphyseon* 697B.
10 MacLeod, 'The Glory in the Grey', in *The Whole Earth*, p. 13.
11 White, 'The Region of Identity', in *The Bird Path*, p. 99.
12 Eriugena, *Periphyseon* 681B
13 A. J. Scott, 'A Lecture on History', *The Manchester Examiner*, 2 October 1847.
14 Eriugena, *Periphyseon* 773C.
15 Eriugena, *Periphyseon* 681A.
16 A. J. Scott, *Two Discourses* (Darling, 1848) p. 36.
17 Eriugena, *Periphyseon* 452C.
18 White, 'The House of Insight', in *The Bird Path*, p. 145.
19 White, 'The House of Insight', in *The Bird Path*, p. 144.
20 MacLeod, 'Man is Made to Rise', in *The Whole Earth*, p. 16.
21 Eriugena, *Periphyseon* 643B.
22 White, 'Walking the Coast', in *The Bird Path*, p. 50.
23 MacLeod, 'The Glory in the Grey', in *The Whole Earth*, p. 14.
24 White, 'Walking the Coast', in *The Bird Path*, p. 51.
25 Eriugena, *Periphyseon* 684A.
26 White, 'The Chaoticist Manifesto', in *The Bird Path*, p. 225.
27 John 1:5.
28 Eriugena, *Periphyseon*, 841D.
29 A. J. Scott, *Suggestions on Female Education* (Maberly, 1849), p. 22.

30 White, 'Valley of Birches', in *The Bird Path*, p. 160.
31 A. Carmichael (ed.), *Carmina Gadelica*, III (Scottish Academic Press, 1976), pp. 111–13.
32 Eriugena, *Periphyseon* 515B.
33 G. MacDonald, *Lilith*, (Eerdmans, 1981), p. 201.
34 A. Carmichael (ed.), *Carmina Gadelica*, I (Constable, 1900), p. 141.
35 G. MacDonald, 'Within and Without', in *The Poetical Works of George MacDonald*, I (Chatto and Windus, 1911), p. 75.

2 *The Second Day: The Wildness of God*

1 Acts 17:28.
2 Genesis 1:2.
3 See Chadwick, *The Celts*, p. 146.
4 MacLeod, 'The Eternal Seeping Through the Physical', in *The Whole Earth*, p. 11.
5 *Carmina Gadelica*, III, p. 231.
6 *Carmina Gadelica*, III, p. 237.
7 Eriugena, *Periphyseon* 554B.
8 Eriugena, *Periphyseon* 555C.
9 Eriugena, *Periphyseon* 554B.
10 MacDonald, *Lilith*, p. 81.
11 MacLeod, 'The Eternal Seeping Through the Physical', in *The Whole Earth*, p. 11.
12 MacLeod, 'A Veil Thin as Gossamer', in *The Whole Earth*, p. 60.
13 Scott, *Lectures on the Epistle to the Romans*, p. 7.
14 Robert Van de Weyer (ed.), *The Letters of Pelagius* (Arthur James, 1995), p. 36.
15 MacDonald, *Lilith*, p. 147.
16 *Carmina Gadelica*, III, p. 143.
17 *Carmina Gadelica*, I, p. 201.
18 *Carmina Gadelica*, I, p. 207.
19 See Luke 19:45 and John 11:35.
20 See Chadwick, *The Celts*, p. 206.
21 Ferguson (ed.), *Daily Readings with George MacLeod*, p. 75.
22 *Carmina Gadelica*, I, p. 3.
23 White, 'Scotia Deserta', in *The Bird Path*, p. 125.
24 White, 'Late August on the Coast', in *The Bird Path*, p. 236.
25 Revelation 10:4.

26 Revelation 1:14–16.
27 *Carmina Gadelica*, I, p. 141.
28 Luke 12:49.
29 Matthew 6:6.

3 The Third Day: The Fecundity of God

1 Eriugena, *Periphyseon* 702C.
2 Genesis 1:12
3 Eriugena, *Periphyseon* 711C.
4 John 1:1, 3.
5 Eriugena, *Periphyseon* 558B.
6 John 1:14.
7 Scott, *Lectures on the Epistle to the Romans*, p. 61.
8 Genesis 1:12.
9 Eriugena, *Periphyseon* 704D.
10 Eriugena, *Periphyseon* 749B.
11 Eriugena, *Periphyseon* 465C.
12 Eriugena, *Periphyseon* 786A.
13 White, 'At the Solstice', in *The Bird Path*, p. 31.
14 Eriugena, *Periphyseon* 470A.
15 Eriugena, *Periphyseon* 628A.
16 Eriugena, *Periphyseon* 628A.
17 Eriugena, *Periphyseon* 511A.
18 See J. P. Newell, 'A. J. Scott and his Circle', PhD Thesis (University of Edinburgh, 1981), p. 346.
19 Exodus 3:5.
20 G. M. Hopkins, 'God's Grandeur', in *Poems and Prose* (Penguin Books, 1953), p. 27.
21 B. R. Rees (ed.), 'Letter to Demetrias', in *The Letters of Pelagius and his Followers* (Boydell, 1991), p. 45.
22 Pelagius, 'On Riches', in *The Letters of Pelagius and his Followers*, p. 183.
23 James 1:17.
24 Pelagius, 'On Riches', in *The Letters of Pelagius and his Followers*, p. 182.
25 Pelagius, 'On Riches', in *The Letters of Pelagius and his Followers*, p. 183.
26 Pelagius, 'On Riches', *The Letters of Pelagius and his Followers*, p. 194.

27 Pelagius, 'On Riches', in *The Letters of Pelagius and his Followers*, p. 191.
28 Pelagius, 'To an Older Friend', in *The Letters of Pelagius and his Followers*, p. 150.
29 Matthew 7:12.
30 Pelagius, 'To Celentia', in *The Letters of Pelagius and his Followers*, pp. 134–35.
31 Pelagius, 'On Virginity', in *The Letters of Pelagius and his Followers*, p. 76.
32 Pelagius, 'On the Christian Life', in *The Letters of Pelagius and his Followers*, p. 124.
33 J. P. Newell (ed.), *The Iona Community Worship Book* (Wild Goose Publications, 1991), p. 27.
34 *Carmina Gadelica*, III, p. 363.
35 Pelagius, 'On the Christian Life', in *The Letters of Pelagius and his Followers*, p. 123.
36 Scott, *The Social Systems of the Present Day*, p. 345.
37 Pelagius, 'To Demetrias', in *The Letters of Pelagius and his Followers*, p. 67.

4 *The Fourth Day: The Harmony of God*

1 Eriugena, *Periphyseon* 711A.
2 Psalm 19:3–4.
3 Eriugena, *Periphyseon* 919A.
4 James 1:17.
5 A. J. Scott, 'On Schism', *The Pulpit* 41 (28 May 1842), p. 511.
6 White, 'The Eight Eccentrics', in *The Bird Path*, p. 137.
7 *Carmina Gadelica*, III, p. 215.
8 *Carmina Gadelica*, III, p. 274.
9 See Colossians 1:17.
10 *Carmina Gadelica*, III, p. 307.
11 *Carmina Gadelica*, III, p. 285.
12 *Carmina Gadelica*, III, p. 209.
13 *Carmina Gadelica*, III, p. 293.
14 *Carmina Gadelica*, III, p. 299.
15 Eriugena, *Periphyseon* 896B.
16 Galatians 3:28.
17 Isaiah 49:15.
18 Malachi 2:10.

19 G. MacDonald, 'The Castle: A Parable', in *The Gifts of the Child Christ*, I (Eerdmans, 1973), p. 290.

20 Scott, *Suggestions on Female Education*, p. 62.

21 Eriugena, *Periphyseon* 533A.

22 Scott, *Two Discourses*, p. 19.

23 *Carmina Gadelica*, I, p. 141.

24 Eriugena, *Periphyseon* 520B.

25 Eriugena, *Periphyseon* 593B.

26 A. J. Scott, 'Self-Education', *The Manchester Examiner and Times*, 18 January 1854.

27 White, 'The House of Insight', in *The Bird Path*, p. 143.

28 White, 'Late August on the Coast', in *The Bird Path*, p. 234.

5 *The Fifth Day: The Creatureliness of God*

1 Eriugena, *Periphyseon* 736B.

2 Eriugena, *Periphyseon* 681A.

3 Eriugena, *Periphyseon* 633A.

4 Eriugena, *Periphyseon* 750A.

5 MacDonald, *Lilith*, p. 248.

6 See H. Richardson, 'Celtic Art', in J. Mackey (ed.), *An Introduction to Celtic Christianity* (Clark, 1989), p. 375.

7 A. J. Scott, 'On Schism', *The Pulpit* 41 (9 June 1842), p. 544.

8 Scott, *Lectures on the Epistle to the Romans*, p. 3.

9 Scott, *Lectures on the Epistle to the Romans*, p. 4.

10 White, 'Walking the Coast', in *The Bird Path*, p. 48.

11 Eriugena, *Periphyseon* 974B.

12 Pelagius, 'To Demetrias', in *The Letters of Pelagius and his Followers*, p. 62.

13 See Ezekiel 1 and I Kings 6:7.

14 Job 12:7.

15 Colossians 1:16.

16 MacDonald, 'The Golden Key', in *The Gifts of the Christ Child*, I, pp. 160–62.

17 White, 'Late August on the Coast', in *The Bird Path*, pp. 237–39.

18 Revelation 4:8.

19 *Carmina Gadelica*, III, p. 25.

20 White, 'Late August on the Coast', in *The Bird Path*, pp. 233–34.

6 *The Sixth Day: The Image of God*

1 Genesis 1:26.
2 MacDonald, *Lilith*, p. 147.
3 Scott, *The Social Systems of the Present Day*, p. 348.
4 Scott, *Two Discourses*, p. 33.
5 Scott, *Lectures on the Epistle to the Romans*, p. 28.
6 A. J. Scott, 'Social Systems', *The Woolwich Gazette*, 2 January 1841.
7 Eriugena, *Periphyseon* 585B.
8 Eriugena, *Periphyseon* 771D.
9 Eriugena, *Periphyseon* 567D.
10 Eriugena, *Periphyseon* 1016B.
11 Pelagius, 'To Demetrias', in *The Letters of Pelagius and his Followers*, p. 39.
12 Romans 2:15.
13 Genesis 3:8–9.
14 Eriugena, *Periphyseon* 822A.
15 Eriugena, *Periphyseon* 841D–842A.
16 Eriugena, *Periphyseon* 962B.
17 Eriugena, *Periphyseon* 777C.
18 Eriugena, *Periphyseon* 919B.
19 Pelagius, 'To Demetrias', in *The Letters of Pelagius and his Followers*, p. 37.
20 MacDonald, *Lilith*, p. 67.
21 MacDonald, *Lilith*, p. 199.
22 A. J. Scott, *On the Divine Will* (Lusk, 1830), p. 11.
23 Psalm 8:5.
24 Isaiah 33:17.
25 Pelagius, 'On Virginity', in *The Letters of Pelagius and his Followers*, p. 84.
26 Pelagius, 'On Virginity', in *The Letters of Pelagius and his Followers*, p. 84.
27 Pelagius, 'To Demetrias', in *The Letters of Pelagius and his Followers*, p. 57.
28 Eriugena, *Periphyseon* 531C.
29 Eriugena, *Periphyseon* 801B.
30 Eriugena, *Periphyseon* 760C.
31 Eriugena, *Periphyseon* 826C.
32 Eriugena, *Periphyseon* 975B.
33 Eriugena, *Periphyseon* 872A–872B.

34 Eriugena, *Periphyseon* 873A.

35 Eriugena, *Periphyseon* 801B.

36 Scott, *Lectures on the Epistle to the Romans*, pp. 76–77.

37 Eriugena, *Periphyseon* 1003C.

38 Scott, *The Social Systems of the Present Day*, p. 375.

39 Pelagius. 'To Demetrias', in *The Letters of Pelagius and his Followers*, p. 45.

40 Eriugena, *Periphyseon* 997B.

41 Pelagius, 'To Demetrias', in *The Letters of Pelagius and his Followers*, p. 54.

42 Hebrews 4:12.

43 MacDonald, *Lilith*, p. 201.

44 MacDonald, *Lilith*, p. 219.

45 Eriugena, *Periphyseon* 956C.

46 Eriugena, *Periphyseon* 1016A.

47 Eriugena, *Periphyseon* 919A.

48 MacDonald, *Lilith*, p. 94.

7 *The Seventh Day: The Stillness of God*

1 A. J. Scott, 'Social Systems', *The Woolwich Gazette*, 2 January 1841.

2 Eriugena, *Periphyseon* 704D.

3 MacDonald, *Lilith*, p. 29.

4 *Carmina Gadelica*, III, p. 333.

5 *Carmina Gadelica*, III, p. 339.

6 Scott, *The Social Systems of the Present Day*, p. 369.

7 Pelagius, 'To Demetrias', in *The Letters of Pelagius and his Followers*, p. 61.

8 Pelagius, 'To Celantia', in *The Letters of Pelagius and his Followers*, p. 140.

9 *Carmina Gadelica*, III, p. 31.

10 *Carmina Gadelica*, I, p. 233.

11 *Carmina Gadelica*, III, p. 33.

12 White, 'The House of Insight', in *The Bird Path*, p. 146.

13 *Carmina Gadelica*, III, pp. 387–89.

14 *Carmina Gadelica*, III, p. 393.

15 MacDonald, *Lilith*, p. 44.

16 MacDonald, *Lilith*, p. 242.

17 MacDonald, *Lilith*, p. 44.

18 *Carmina Gadelica*, III, pp. 383–85.